M000192384

IS THE NEGRO A BEAST?

A REPLY TO
CHAS. CARROLL'S BOOK
ENTITLED
"THE NEGRO A BEAST."

Proving that the Negro is Human from Biblical,
Scientific, and Historical Standpoints.

———

BY

WM. G. SCHELL.

Author of "Biblical Trace of the Church," "The Better Testament," "The Ordinances of the New Testament," etc.

———

MOUNDSVILLE, W. VA., U. S. A.
GOSPEL TRUMPET PUBLISHING COMPANY.
1901.

This scarce antiquarian book is included in our special *Legacy Reprint Series*. In the interest of creating a more extensive selection of rare historical book reprints, we have chosen to reproduce this title even though it may possibly have occasional imperfections such as missing and blurred pages, missing text, poor pictures, markings, dark backgrounds and other reproduction issues beyond our control. Because this work is culturally important, we have made it available as a part of our commitment to protecting, preserving and promoting the world's literature.

CONTENTS.

LIST OF ILLUSTRATIONS.

6

PREFACE.

During many centuries of the world's history a custom prevailed in many of the nations of the earth of employing bond men and bond women for the performance of common labor. The first appearance of slavery in the western world of which we have any record was during the sixteenth century, when the Spaniards took possession of Central America, Mexico, and the West Indies, robbing its native inhabitants—the American Indians—of their rightful wealth and possessions, and reducing them to bondage and servitude. In the space of forty years twelve millions of these people were worked to death in the mines, and otherwise suffered premature death, at the hands of the merciless and barbarous Spaniards. Whole cities and scores of towns were thus depopulated. This cruel practice continued until the excitement resulting from the discovery of excessive wealth in the western continent had abated.

The question of slavery was but lightly considered in what now constitutes the United States of America, prior to the year 1619, when the captain of a Dutch

7

trading vessel sold twenty African Negroes as slaves
to some of the plantation settlers at Jamestown, Virginia.   Their value as laborers was readily discerned,
and expeditions were soon fitted out for the purpose
of bringing these people from their native home in
Africa to the wilds of America, to be thenceforth servants unto the white man.   After the plantations of
Virginia were supplied with Negroes, the practice of
buying and selling them was extended throughout
several states of the South.   Families of the despised
blacks were broken up and relatives scattered, and the
wretched unfortunates entertained but little hope of
ever meeting again on earth.   This inhuman traffic—
dealing in the souls and bodies of men and women—
was perpetrated for more than two hundred years,
until abolished by the pen of Abraham Lincoln in his
memorable Emancipation Proclamation at the city of
Washington, January first, eighteen hundred sixty-
three, and a subsequent amendment to the Constitution, declaring slavery forever abolished in all territory
within the jurisdiction of the United States of
America.

The hearts of true Christians everywhere, and of all
others who are not imbued with a deadly race prejudice,
are caused to gratefully adore and thank the Creator
of all for the liberation of this poor, despised, and

persecuted race of people. And now in the brilliant sunlight of modern intellectual development and civilization, "We hold these truths to be self-evident: that all men are created *equal;* that they are endowed by their Creator with certain inalienable rights; that among these are life, *liberty*, and the pursuit of happiness." But hark! from the distance I hear a voice, loud and clear, whose echoes resound throughout the length and breadth of the land, exclaiming: "The entire world is in error; the Negro is not a man, he is simply a beast; read my book entitled 'The Negro a Beast,'—'The revelation of the century.' " It is the voice of Charles Carroll.

This author makes a desperate effort in the above-mentioned book to substantiate his theory that the Negro is not human, and possesses no immortal soul, but is simply a "black biped beast," and therefore only intended for a slave. This he professes to prove by a correct interpretation of Holy Writ and in accordance with the latest researches of modern science. Accepting as an hypothesis that the Negro is a beast, Mr. Carroll endeavors to harmonize the Bible and science with his position. After a careful examination of the book entitled "The Negro a Beast," Mr. William G. Schell, who is a minister of the gospel, *feels it his* duty to place before the reading public a work on the subject, in reply to the position assumed by Prof. Carroll, showing wherein he has shamefully misrepresented and wrested the Holy Scriptures, and proving his self-manufactured *science* to be nothing but "science, falsely so-called." This is the only necessary apology for the appearance of the present work. The theories propounded by Mr. Carroll vanish from our sight into the realm of obscurity and darkness, whence they emanated, before the convincing arguments of this book.

May God hasten the time when all race prejudice may be obliterated, and every soul for whom Christ died be recognized as precious in his sight, and a worthy recepient of the redemption grace purchased in the death of our Savior.   F. G. SMITH.

Moundsville, W. Va., Nov. 12, 1901.

Is the Negro a Beast?

INTRODUCTION.

SINCE I have read Charles Carroll's new book entitled "The Negro a Beast," I have carefully examined his proof texts, and am driven to say by facts that force themselves into my mind, that our author has drawn wrong conclusions from the texts of scripture he cites as proofs of his theory. If my conclusions can be substantiated, his theory is basely false, and is left to fall by the weight of its own falsity, as far as scriptural proofs are concerned.

Mr. Carroll has failed to make it clear to my mind that the Negro is a beast created by God to be a servant unto man. His book throughout seems to convict him of the crime of studying the sacred volume to prove a preconceived idea. In this way any man might, in defense of any erroneous notion, spin out a tiny thread of something that would appear to the ignorant as strongest evidence. But such seeming evidence melts away before the mind that has been trained to study the Bible to know what it teaches, like morning dew before the rising sun.

Many who read "The Negro a Beast" will throw it aside in disgust, feeling that the misconstructions of scripture are so clearly discernible that a refutation will not be needed. But I do not view this book exactly in that light, because there are many people in America who are uninformed in regard to scriptural teachings; in fact, few of them ever acquired a thorough knowledge of the Bible, and those who have not are generally so careless that they never examine a proof text quoted by an author, nor its context. Such people Mr. Carroll's volume is well calculated to deceive, particularly so if they are possessed with the race prejudice that rages so highly in many parts of the country. In view of these facts, I feel it extremely necessary that a work should be placed before the public, that will overturn all the wrestings of scripture found in Mr. Carroll's book, and stop the mouths of "vain talkers" who would try to make it appear that our brother in black is an "evil beast."

Mr. Carroll claims to have spent fifteen years in the preparation of his book. I would suggest that it would have been *far better* if he had spent fifteen years more in careful consideration of his theory before he published his book. He is dabbling into things of vast importance, and advancing ideas upon which are hinged more perhaps than he is aware of. A false theory based upon false premises and erroneous arguments is like so many poisonous snakes turned loose among the innocent and uninformed people. They and their progenitors will continue ever creeping around among the masses and occasionally, if not frequently, inflicting a poisonous bite in some unsuspecting soul. And should he who turned them loose become convinced that his theory is wrong, it will be impossible for him to ever catch all the poisonous reptiles and sack them up again. Though his theory should die—as such theories often do—with the generation in which it is born, the poisonous ideas connected with the same will follow some souls to the judgment of the great day to come.

It would mean a great deal for us to accept Mr. Carroll's theory. It would drive us to the belief that the line of distinction between the human family and lower animals is so obscure that in thousands of years there was never a scientist capable of marking it out. It would compel us to exterminate all the various colors of creatures that in form and appearance resemble both the white man and Mr. Carroll's black beast, because he says "the mixed-bloods have no right to live." If they have no right to live, they ought to be killed, and we as men should destory all the mixed-bloods and place the black beast in the place where he belongs; namely, a servant and a slave unto man. Such is exactly the doctrine of Mr. Carroll. And he states emphatically in his book that if the people of the South had held their slaves as apes and beasts, instead of human beings, there would have been no power to have them taken from them. Oh, shame on such a reviler of civilization in these days! Shame on the man who feign would murder half of the human family under the crazy notion that they are satyrs, hobgoblins, or some mixture of man and beast! And I say also, Shame on the man who can not tell a man from a beast by the sense of sight alone!

Mr. Carroll's boast is that the doctrine he advocates has never been replied to, and never will be refuted; and he seems inclined to brand everything written against his idea as ridicule. Of course I agree with him that ridicule is not argument, neither shall I in the following pages spend my time ridiculing his theory. I intend to follow his notions one by one and examine the texts he quotes from the Bible as proof texts, and show by common sense interpretation that he has twisted them. Of course I may at times give him a little plain talk such as he justly merits. And how can I, seeing the abuses of God's holy word that he puts out before the public, avoid denouncing his atrocious crime in the strongest terms?

I do not intend to write a book without leaving traces of my fallibility; I am not infallible: but I am certain that I shall be able by the help of God to show many reasons why Mr. Carroll's theory is as false as the doctrine of polygamy, and as abominable in the sight of God as the doctrine of the Nicolaitanes. I am certain that he misunderstands God's plan of creation; he misunderstands the plan of redemption; he misunderstands science; and he misunderstands the Bible throughout, as far as pertains to his theory. With these preliminary remarks I will proceed to the subject.

MR. CARROLL'S THEORY OF CREATION.

Mr. CARROLL sums up his theory of creation as follows: "Thus the long-lost knowledge of the three creations, matter, mind, and soul, are restored to us, and the beautiful unfolding of God's plan of redemption as set forth in the Mosaic record is clearly revealed. First. Matter, created in the beginning, the basis of all form aion, the material out of which all bodies are formed. Second. Mind, a new element which made its appearance in the material universe on the fifth day, in combination with matter, as presented in the physical organism of the fish. Third. Soul, a new element which made its appearance in the material universe on the sixth day, in combination with matter and with mind, as presented in the physical and mental organisms of man."—p. 370.

The reader will observe that Mr. Carroll here divides God's creation into three parts; or, in other words, he shows that God used his creative power three times while he was forming this world and all things pertaining to it. His idea of the three creations he bases upon the use made of the word create in the record Moses gives us of the creation of the world.

That the reader may understand him more clearly, I will quote the three texts containing the word create.

"In the beginning God created the heaven and the earth. And the earth was without form, and void." —Gen. 1:1, 2.

"And God said, Let the waters bring forth abundantly the moving creature that hath life [*Hebrew, soul* —Margin], and fowl that may fly above the earth in the open firmament of heaven. And God created great whales, and every living creature that moveth, which the waters brought forth abundantly, after their kind, and every winged fowl after his kind: and God saw that it was good. . . . And the evening and the morning were the fifth day."—Gen. 1:20-23.

"And God said, Let us make man in our image, after our likeness: and let them have dominion over the fish of the sea, and over the fowl of the air, and over the cattle, and over all the earth, and over every creeping thing that creepeth upon the earth. So God created man in his own image, in the image of God created he him; male and female created he them."—Gen. 1:26, 27.

Since the Bible does not use the word create in the record of the creation except in these three instances,

Carroll is certainly right in regard to the use of creative power three times in the formation of the world and all it contains. But he certainly does not possess the correct idea of the new elements God brought into existence in each of these three creations. I agree with him that God spoke into existence in the beginning the elements of matter out of which he fashioned the material world and all that it contained down to the fifth day; for it does not appear that he used creative power on the first, second, third, and fourth days. The records of the events of these days show that God merely commanded the division of the land from the waters, and the grass, herbs, trees, etc., to spring out of the matter he had created in the beginning. We have an unanswerable proof in the second chapter of Genesis that vegetable life was brought out of the matter created in the beginning, and that no additional creative power was employed in its formation. The words I refer to are these: "These are the generations of the heavens and of the earth when they were created, in the day that the Lord God made the earth and the heavens, and every plant of the field before it was in the earth, and every herb of the field before it grew." —Verses 4, 5. If God created every plant and herb of the field before it grew, it is evident that the making of them on the third day was not a creation, but a making.

out of things formerly created. In this manner all the works of the first four days were accomplished.

But when we come to animal life on the fifth day, we find the exercising of a power greater than the molding of something out of elements previously spoken into existence. We find it written, "And God *created* great whales and every living creature that moveth, which the waters brought forth," etc. In this instance God formed creatures out of elements he had caused to exist in the beginning, but he added new elements, which he at that time spoke into existence. This must be true, since the word create means to cause to exist. But what was the newly created element that was essential to animal life? Carroll says it was mind. I take no exceptions: for there certainly is proof that animals possess mind to some extent, but not to the extent that our author believes.

We now come to the making of man. God formed him out of the dust of the ground. From this it is evident that God made man in part of the elements that he had spoken into existence in the beginning and on the fifth day. But he added a newly created element, for we are told that God created man; therefore man must contain some element that was not contained in the creation of anything made prior to the sixth day. What was this newly created element that was essential

to the formation of man? Carroll says it was soul. I
think not; because the Hebrew of Gen. 1:20 shows
that the animals created on the fifth day possessed souls
as well as a corporeal body. And it appears from a
careful study of this text that incorporeal counterparts
of the bodies of animals were formed from elements
that had been spoken into existence in the beginning.
The word create, therefore, applied to the formation
of animal life, must refer, as Carroll says, to the mind
that is essential to its existence. With these thoughts
in our mind, let us look at the formation of man.

God formed man as he formed the lower animals;
that is, he formed him out of the elements that had
been spoken into existence in the two previous creations; viz., in the beginning, and on the fifth day:
that is, he formed man's body, soul, and mind out of
that which had been previously created. What, therefore, was the newly created element God used in the
formation of man? The best explanation of this is
found in the words, "God . . . breathed into his nostrils
the breath of life; and man became a living soul."—
Gen. 2:7. *Breath* in this text is from *neshamah*, which
is the word used for spirit in Prov. 20:27, which says,
"The spirit of man is the candle of the Lord." So it
appears that it was the spirit of man that God created
in the formation of man. The spirit and soul of man

are often confounded, but there is a distinction drawn between them in the Bible. Heb. 4:12 tells us that "the word of God is quick, and powerful, and sharper than any two-edged sword, piercing even to the dividing asunder of soul and spirit." From this text it appears that the soul and spirit are not the same. In 1 Thess. 5:23 the apostle says, "I pray God your whole spirit and soul and body be preserved blameless unto the coming of our Lord Jesus Christ." This text can not be explained without we make a distinction between the soul and the spirit of man.

So, to return to the creation, we must conclude (since the original Hebrew in Gen. 1:20 shows that the lower animals possess souls, and Ver. 21 shows that God created a new element in the formation of animals, which was undoubtedly mind) that God formed the soul, mind, and body of man out of elements he had spoken into existence in the beginning and on the fifth day. The soul of man thus formed would have been mortal, and in no sense superior to the soul of animals but for the infusion of a newly created element by God into man, which changed the soul and mind of man into an immortal state. We must therefore make the following distinctions between man and the lower animals: The soul of man is immortal; while the soul *of the beast is mortal.* The mind of man is immortal;

while the mind of the beast is mortal. Therefore we must not say that animals possess in any degree the same mind that man possesses; because that which they possess has not been immortalized, while the mind of man has. This may be proven by the accounts given in the Scriptures of disembodied souls, from which we learn that they possess mind the same as when in their embodied state. We read of three of them in Luke 16:19-31, which I quote.

"There was a certain rich man, which was clothed in purple and fine linen, and fared sumptuously every day: and there was a certain beggar named Lazarus, which was laid at his gate, full of sores, and desiring to be fed with the crumbs which fell from the rich man's table: moreover the dogs came and licked his sores. And it came to pass, that the beggar died, and was carried by the angels into Abraham's bosom: the rich man also died, and was buried; and in hell he lift up his eyes, being in torments, and seeth Abraham afar off, and Lazarus in his bosom. And he cried and said, Father Abraham, have mercy on me, and send Lazarus, that he may dip the tip of his finger in water, and cool my tongue; for I am tormented in this flame. But Abraham said, Son, remember that thou in thy lifetime receivedst thy good things, and likewise Lazarus evil things: but now he is comforted and thou

THE RICH MAN, AND LAZARUS IN ABRAHAM'S BOSOM.

art tormented. And beside all this, between us and you there is a great gulf fixed: so that they which would pass from hence to you can not; neither can they pass to us, that would come from thence. Then he said, I pray thee therefore, father, that thou wouldest send him to my father's house: for I have five brethren; that he may testify unto them, lest they also come into this place of torment. Abraham saith unto him, They have Moses and the prophets; let them hear them. And he said, Nay, father Abraham: but if one went unto them from the dead, they will repent. And he said unto him, If they hear not Moses and the prophets, neither will they be persuaded, though one rose from the dead."

This is a clear record of three dead men. The rich man possessed the sense of sight, because he looked across a great gulf and saw Lazarus. He, as well as Abraham, possessed the knowledge of language and ability to use the organs of speech, as well as the sense of hearing, because they held a conversation. They both possessed memory also, because they talked about circumstances connected with the rich man's life upon earth. Both Lazarus and the rich man possessed consciousness and the sense of feeling, because the former was comforted, and the latter tormented. These are undeniable proofs that the mind of man is immortal and lives with the soul after death.

Under the opening of the fifth seal the Revelator "saw under the altar the souls of them that were slain for the word of God, and for the testimony which they held: and they cried with a loud voice, saying, How long, O Lord, holy and true, dost thou not judge and avenge our blood on them that dwell on the earth? And white robes were given unto every one of them; and it was said unto them, that they should rest yet for a little season, until their fellow-servants also and their brethren, that should be killed as they were, should be fulfilled."—Rev. 6:9-11.   This is a strange story about departed souls, if the mind of man is not immortal and does not live with the soul after death.

Surely the reader can not fail to see that the mind of man is different from the mind of animals, in that it is a deathless entity; while the mind of animals is mortal, and dies with the body. So Mr. Carroll's theory is wrong, in that it makes the mind of animals and the mind of man the same in essence.   This could not be true, except the mind of man were mortal, which we have disproved, or the mind of animals were immortal, which can not be true, because they possess no deathless entity.   The fact that mind always accompanies the disembodied soul in the inspired records, proves that it as well as the soul was rendered immortal by the infusion of spirit into man at his creation. Therefore, only those creatures which possess immortal souls can possess the immortal mind; and only those which possess immortal minds can possess immortal souls. The weight of argument, therefore, so far as this question pertains to the Negro, lies in the matter of the possession by him of an immortal mind and an immortal soul. If it can be shown that the Negro possesses an immortal mind, it will have been proven that he possesses an immortal soul; and since only man possesses an immortal soul, to prove that the Negro possesses an immortal soul is to prove that he is a man.

To show that the Negro possesses an immortal mind, I will draw some distinctions between mind immortal and mind mortal. All mind, both mortal and immortal, possesses the consciousness of existence, but mind immortal possesses the consciousness of existence after death; while mind mortal possesses no such consciousness. It has been demonstrated that the most insignificant species of animals possess consciousness of existence, but it has never been demonstrated that the consciousness of future existence exists in any of the lower animals—man only possesses this.

That the consciousness of future existence is a proper product of the human mind, is evident from the fact that the human family universally have held to the

belief of a future existence in all ages, no difference
how deeply they were sunken into degradation and
barbarism. Even in dark Africa, where the poor
Negroes live, the belief of a future existence prevails
among the most degraded tribes. Of these, Thomas
Dick, in his "Philosophy of the Future State," says:

"The various tribes which inhabit the continent of
Africa, in so far as we are acquainted with their religious opinions, appear to recognize the doctrine of a
future state. 'I was lately discoursing on this subject,'
says Mr. Addison, in one of his Spectators, 'with a
learned person, who has been very much conversant
among the inhabitants of the most western parts of
Africa. Upon his conversing with several in that
country, he tells me, he found that their notion of
heaven or of a future state of happiness, is this: that
everything we there wish for will immediately present
itself to us. We find, say they, that our souls are of
such a nature that they require variety, and are not capable of always being delighted with the same objects.
The Supreme Being, therefore, in compliance with this
state of happiness which he has implanted in the soul
of man, will raise up, from time to time, say they,
every gratification which it is in the human nature to
be pleased with. If we wish to be in groves or bowers,
among running streams or falls of water, we shall im-

mediately find ourselves in the midst of such a scene as we desire. If we would be entertained with music and the melody of sounds, the concert arises upon our wish, and the whole region about us is filled with harmony. In short, every desire will be followed by fruition; and whatever a man's inclination directs him to, will be present with him.' The Negroes, and other inhabitants of the interior of Africa, according to the account of Mr. Park, believe in one Supreme Ruler, and expect hereafter to enter into a state of misery or felicity."

According to these words of Dick, the Negro, as well as other heathen tribes, possess the belief in a future state. Whence has he this belief but from his inward consciousness? If he were an ape, as Mr. Carroll states, he would, when separated from the society of man for hundreds of years, retain no belief in a future state; but would, like the ape, live and move only for the present. But he as firmly believes in the future state as does the Christian, and since he is without the light of God's word, we must attribute his belief in the future state to an inward consciousness. The consciousness of future existence being a prerogative of man, we have in this an unanswerable proof that the Negro is a man.

There is another prerogative of the human mind. It

is natural for the mind of man to worship. In all the world there are no tribes who do not manifest a consciousness of a higher power. Although in many places the barbarous tribes possess very poor ideas of that Supreme Being, they nevertheless possess the consciousness that there is a God of some kind, and are endeavoring to render worship to him. Animals possess no such worshipful natures. They possess no consciousness of the existence of a God. The Negroes and all the colored nations in a barbarous state possess the consciousness of the existence of a God. This would not be true in regard to them if they did not possess the mind of man, for apes are not capable of even learning this fact. But the Negro as well as the white man possesses both the consciousness of the existence of a God and the consciousness of his future existence. These are prerogatives of man, and the fact that they exist in the Negro proves him a man.

In his zeal to defend his theory, which teaches that the mind of animals and the mind of man are the same in essence, our author affirms on pages 120-128 of his book, that the animals as well as men possess the moral faculty. He says it is the moral faculty in the animal which makes it possible for men to teach them that it is right to obey, and wrong to disobey their master. I must here again differ with Mr. Carroll. It is not the moral faculty in animals which makes it possible for us to govern them. There is no proof that animals obey men because they think it their moral duty. They must either be coaxed or terrified into submission. The moral faculty in man is that which renders it possible to bring him under a conviction of right, by means of which he will of himself perform right deeds.

When we examine the Bible description of the moral faculty, it is then that the position of our author appears ridiculous. Paul describes it as follows: "For when the Gentiles, which have not the law, do by nature the things contained in the law, these, having not the law, are a law unto themselves: which show the work of the law written in their hearts, their conscience also bearing witness, and their thoughts the meanwhile accusing or else excusing one another."— Rom. 2:14, 15.

According to this text the moral faculty is the law of God written in the heart. All the moral laws of God were inscribed in the heart of man in the creation; hence doing right at that time was a natural consequence. These moral laws have been partially effaced from the human heart by sin, but in all men, though in the lowest state of degradation, there are some remaining traces of God's moral law. There is no

totally depraved heart.   This moral law within man is
the moral faculty.   It is not the knowledge of right,
but the nature of right.   It is the remains of the moral
law in man that causes him to realize that he is a being subject to moral law, and accuses him when he has
performed evil deeds, and excuses him when he has
done good deeds.

If animals possess the moral faculty, they have the
moral laws of God written in their hearts, and, of
course, must feel accused when they perform bad
deeds, and excused when they perform good deeds.
Think of the compunctions of conscience a horse feels
after he has kicked you! or what dreadful remorse of
conscience a dog will suffer under after he has bitten
you! This must be a true description of lower animals,
if they possess the moral faculty, as Carroll states.   I
wonder if he does not believe also that the animals have
in some way participated in the fall, and that they at
the present time have the moral laws of God partially
effaced from their nature? If so, he would make a
good advocate of that branch of the Millennial theory
which teaches the redemption of animals in a fancied
age to come.   It seems to me that our author's theory
would require an extension of the atonement to include
the rewriting of the law of God in animals, the same
as in man.   See Heb. 8:10.   But the Bible teaches no

such things. Mr. Carroll is mistaken. Only man possesses the moral faculty; only man has a conscience, and suffers under its compunctions, is capable of sinning, and is included in the atonement.

The Negro possesses the moral faculty the same as the Caucasian. This our author will not dare to deny. But instead of frankly acknowledging this fact a proof that the Negro possesses the same immortal mind that the Caucasian possesses, and is therefore a man, he employs the twist that all the lower animals possess the moral faculty, and that therefore the existence of the moral faculty in the Negro is no proof that he is a man. He has surely taken a long road to get around the truth in this case; but he will find it so broad that he will be unable to walk around it. It will always confront him and cross his pathway; and unless he changes his course, he will die in his efforts to get around this truth. So, after a careful consideration of Mr. Carroll's theory, reason compels me to throw it overboard and to continue to look upon my brother in black in the same light that I looked upon him before I read Mr. Carroll's "Revelation (?) of the Century."

MR. CARROLL'S BLACK BIPED BEAST—
A MYTH.

ANOTHER feature of Mr. Carroll's creation theory
is that the Negro was created before man, to be a
servant unto man. To substantiate this theory he
claims the Negro to be the beast mentioned in the following text: "And God said, Let the earth bring forth
the living creature after his kind, cattle, and creeping
thing, and beast of the earth after his kind: and it was
so."—Gen. 1:24.

A few of Mr. Carroll's comments upon this text will
give the reader a correct idea of his theory. "This
division of the land animals into three classes, named
cattle, creeping things, and beast, is observed throughout the Scriptures. . . . The distinction which God
makes between cattle and beast is based upon the differences in their physical structure. The cattle are
quadrupeds, the beasts are bipeds—apes. . . . Observe
the distinction made between the cattle and the
beast of the field, and that in this statement the fowls
are placed between the cattle and beast of the field,

Theologians pay little or no attention to the beast of the field, and seem to take it for granted that the beasts of the field are that class of animals which are designed to be harnessed to the beam and draw the plow. But a careful investigation of this subject reveals the startling truth that this was the creature whom God designed to grasp the handles and direct the team. . . . The Negro made his appearance upon the earth as the beast of the earth and is sometimes referred to by that name. When Adam named the animals he named the Negro the beast of the field, and this name is generally applied to him in scripture, although he is frequently referred to simply as beast.'' —Pages 197-203.

To accept Mr. Carroll's doctrine we must accept changes not only in theology, but also in language. He introduces an entirely new use of the word *beast*. He makes it a designation of a particular class of animals. This I am sure is foreign to any use of that word in ancient or modern times. If the original word translated *beast* in Gen. 1:24 signifies a particular kind of animal, the word *beast* is an improper translation of the term, because it has no such signification in our language. Webster's definition of the word *beast* is as follows:

"Any four-footed animal which may be used for

labor, food or support, as opposed to man; any
irrational animal."

Alden's Manifold Cyclopædia defines this word as
follows: "Any four-footed animal; a person rude,
coarse, and filthy."

The Standard Dictionary defines it 1. "An animal,
especially one of the larger quadrupeds, or one that
arouses fear or repulsion, commonly opposed to man,
and excluding birds, fishes and invertebrals. 2. A
draft or riding animal, as a horse or mule. 3. A
beast, cow, or other animal domesticated on a farm.
4. A brutal, rude, or filthy person. 5. A game of
cards resembling loo. 6. Any animal or living being."

These authorities give us all the meanings of the
word *beast* in our language. The word is properly applied to any four-footed animal, and is always applied
to lower animals, except, in a metaphoric sense, to
persons, rude, coarse, or filthy, or when used in a
scientific sense as a synonym of *animal.* It is applied
both to domestic and wild beasts, to beasts of burden,
and beasts used for food; but it will not admit the application Mr. Carroll makes of it.

If Mr. Carroll wants to establish the idea that the
word *beast* in the text before us signifies a Negro, he
has gone at it in the wrong way. Instead of introduc-
ing a definition of the word for which he has no author-

ity, he should have begun at the original and corrected the translation by the use of a word in our language that properly signifies the Negro. If he had endeavored to prove that the original would justify the word Negro in the translation, rather than beast, he would have had a more sensible theory, but would nevertheless have been in error, because the original would not admit such a translation. The Hebrew word *chai* can not be made to designate a particular kind of ape, as he makes the Negro. In the Septuagint, or LXX., which is the oldest Greek translation of the Old Testament, and in fact the oldest translation from the Hebrew into any language, dating back 285 B. C., this word is translated by the word *therion*, which signifies a wild beast. This gives a very sensible interpretation of the text, which, according to the use of this word in the LXX., should be translated, "Let the earth bring forth the living creature after his kind, cattle, and creeping thing, and wild beast of the earth after his kind: and it was so."

The word *cattle* designates the domesticated animals, as the following definitions from standard authors show. CATTLE. 1. "Domesticated bovine animals, as oxen, cows, bulls, and calves; also, though seldom now as compared with former times, any live stock kept for use or profit, as horses, camels, sheep, goats,

swine, etc. In the time of Chaucer and Wyclif
cattle was used in the sense of wealth or substance
generally; whereas now its equivalent, cattle, is only
used to express property in living animals, the form
chattel being reserved for non-living property. 2.
Human beings, said contemptuously. 3. Chattel,
chattels, property."—Standard Dictionary.

CATTLE. 1. "Domesticated quadrupeds collectively,
especially those of the bovine genus, sometimes also
including sheep, goats, horses, mules, asses and swine.
2. Animals; persons (rare)."—Webster.

These authorities give the use of the word cattle in
every sense in our language, even the obsolete application of this term to include both cattle and chattel as
we now understand these terms. But these definitions
will not admit the application of the word cattle
to wild beasts; it can be applied only to domesticated
animals. Therefore Mr. Carroll's theory that the
Negro is the beast of the text before us can not be
true, from the fact that we can not include the wild
carnivorous animals of the forest in the word cattle;
which we must do if the word beast designates the
Negro. The word cattle is the only other word in
that text under which we could include the wild
animals. So if we would translate this text according
to Mr. Carroll's theory, it would read as follows: "And

God said, Let the earth bring forth the living creature
after his kind, animals for domestication, and creeping
thing, and the negro after his kind: and it was so."
There would be no wild beasts in the text, and if they
had not been in this text they would not have been in
the world. So the fact that they are in the world
proves that they have a place somewhere in this text
which mentions the creation of all living creatures
except man. If we translate this text according to the
translation of the word *chai* in the LXX., the text
would read: "And God said, Let the earth bring forth
the living creature after his kind, beasts for domestication, and creeping thing, and wild beasts of the earth
after his kind: and it was so." This gives a translation that is sensible and harmonious with language
ancient and modern, and finds room in the text for
every kind of living creature, and must therefore give
the correct idea.

The placing of the "creeping thing" between cattle
and beast in the text is not of the importance that Mr.
Carroll thinks; because in the next verse the enumera-
tion is different, and places the creeping thing after the
mention of the beast of the earth and the cattle.

There are many reasons why the Negro can not be
the beast of the earth that God created before he
created man. First. He is styled the "beast of the

field" in Gen. 2:19. This expression is not a name given to the Negro by Adam, as our author thinks, but is applied to the lower animals, to describe in some sense their nature and character. They are called beasts of the field because they were designed to live and subsist in the field and feed by grazing. We are shown in Gen. 1:30 that God gave the green herbs to the beasts of the earth, the fowl of the air, and the creeping thing, for meat. I am sure that there is nothing about the Negro that would indicate that he has ever been capable of graminivorous habits. His physical form in every way indicates that he is to feed in the same manner as the Caucasian, and can not be driven into the fields and subsist. How then could he be styled the beast of the field?

Another reason why the Negro can not be the beast of the field, is that the inspired records show that this term is a designation of various species. The word every in connection with this expression is used many times in Genesis, as follows: "Every beast of the earth."—Gen. 1:30. "Every beast of the field."—Gen. 2:19. "Every beast of the field."—Gen. 3:14. If the "beast of the field" designated the Negro, why would the Bible speak of "every beast of the field" in those early days? If God created such a black creature and styled him "beast of the field," he surely created

ADAM NAMING THE BEASTS AND BIRDS.—*Carroll*.

but one pair; how then could the inspired record speak of God·bringing "every beast of the field" before Adam to see what he would name them? Does not this language clearly imply that there were various species of animals that were called "beasts of the field"? Observe also that in Gen. 2:19, where the Bible tells us that the Lord formed out of the ground "every beast of the field and every fowl of the air," and brought them unto Adam to see what he would call them, no words are used to designate any living creature except beast and fowl. Therefore, if the beast mentioned there were the Negro, it could not be proven that God brought any creatures before Adam to receive names, but Negroes and birds. This idea I must say is grossly ridiculous. It is very evident that the domestic and wild animals can not be included in the word fowl, and if they are included in this text at all they must be included in the word beast. · And it is evident that they are included in the word beast, because in the next verse we read, "And Adam gave names to all the cattle, and to all the fowl of the air, and to every beast of the field." So the cattle of the twentieth verse are included with the beasts of the field in the nineteenth verse. This sets forth these words just as we understand their meaning in our language to-day. The word *beast may signify* both domestic and wild beasts; but the word cattle signifies only the domestic. When God recites to us an account of his creation he distinguishes between the domestic and wild beasts, by the use of two words; but when he speaks of bringing these creatures before Adam to be named he lumps them all off together and calls them "every beast of the field." After they are named he distinguishes again by the use of the same two words that he used when giving us an account of the creation; for he says, "Adam gave names to all the cattle, and to the fowl of the air, and to every beast of the field." In this place again the LXX. employs the word *therion*, or wild beasts. So Adam really gave names to all the cattle; that is, the horses, asses, camels, sheep, cows, etc.: and he also gave names to all the wild beasts; the lions, tigers, foxes, wolves, bears, elephants, etc. And he named all the birds of every species; but he did not name any Negroes, because he happened not to have any.

There is yet another reason why the Negro can not be the beast of the field mentioned in Genesis. In the seventh chapter of this book we read of God instructing Noah concerning what manner of creatures should be taken into the ark with him to preserve the seed. The command is as follows: "Of every clean beast thou shalt take to thee by seven, the male and his

ENTERING THE ARK.—*Carroll's Theory.*

female: and of beasts that are not clean by two, the male and his female. Of fowls also of the air by sevens, the male and female; to keep seed alive upon the face of all the earth."—Verses 2, 3. The reader will bear in mind that Mr. Carroll says in the words we cited from him in the beginning of this chapter, that God named the Negro beast when he created him, and that Adam gave him the name of "beast of the field." He also stated that the Negro is sometimes called by the name "beast of the field," but is generally denominated simply "beast." Therefore, according to his teaching, God's command to Noah concerning the lower animals was that he should only take into the ark Negroes and birds; for the term beast is used here, which, according to Mr. Carroll, is the general scriptural designation of the Negro. Noah took into the ark seven clean Negroes, and two unclean Negroes, and a lot of birds. This is exactly according to Mr. Carroll's theory. If he be right, the tradition that Noah took with him into the ark a pair of every kind of four-footed beast, is erroneous. He preserved nothing of the lower animals but Negroes and birds! The cows, horses, camels, asses, lions, tigers, elephants, etc., were every one of them drowned in the flood! But sensible men would like to have Mr. Carroll state how they managed to resist the flood and preserve

themselves alive down to the present day.   Mr. Carroll
may say this is only ridicule, but I insist that it is
more.   It is a fair test of his doctrine.

If we drop down to the thirteenth verse we will find
the key to the word beast as used by God in his command to Noah.   "In the selfsame day entered Noah,
and Shem, and Ham, and Japeth, the sons of Noah,
and Noah's wife, and the three wives of his sons with
them, into the ark; they, and every beast after his
kind, and all the cattle after their kind, and every
creeping thing that creepeth upon the earth after his
kind, and every fowl after his kind, every bird of every
sort."   In this verse we have the beast divided into
there classes· viz., beasts, cattle, and creeping things.
Here again we have *therion*—wild beasts—in the LXX.
So the word beast in God's command to Noah included
all the wild beasts, and all the cattle—domestic beasts
—and all the creeping things.   This is an unanswerable
proof that the Negro is not the beast mentioned in the
book of Genesis.

If we turn to Gen. 8:20 we see why it was that Noah
took with him into the ark seven of every kind of clean
beasts and birds, while he took only a pair of every
unclean species.   There concerning Noah after he came
out of the ark, we read: "And Noah builded an altar
unto the Lord; and took of every clean beast, and of

NOAH'S SACRIFICE, ACCORDING TO CARROLL'S ARGUMENT.

every clean fowl, and offered burnt offerings on the altar." If Mr. Carroll's theory were true we should be compelled to believe that some of the poor Negroes were offered in sacrifice on the altar with some birds. But of course his theory is not true. The clean beasts were such as were considered proper sacrifices to God. They were doubtless such as oxen, sheep, and goats.

MR. CARROLL'S TWISTS UNTWISTED.

IN the chapter entitled "The Beast is a Biped Animal, Not a Quadruped," Mr. Carroll cites many texts of scripture from which he earnestly endeavors by certain twists to prove his false theory, tnat the. Negro is the beast spoken of in the Old Testament. All the texts he cites he most wretchedly twists, and it is my intention to show under this heading wherein he has twisted them, and set them before the public in their true light.

One of the texts he twists is Gen. 9:2—"And the fear of you and the dread of you shall be upon every beast of the earth, and upon every fowl of the air, upon all that moveth upon the earth, and upon all the fishes of the sea; into your hand are they delivered." Commenting upon this text Mr. Carroll says: "God thus names (1) the beast of the earth; (2) the fowl of the air; (3) all that moveth upon the earth; (4) the fish of the sea. Thus we see that in this statement the beast of the earth is separated from the rest of the land animals by the fowl of the air. Thus it is shown that the beast of the earth is not a general term applying

to the carnivora, but is the name of a particular race
of the beast or ape species."—Page 200.

The reader will observe the nature of the twist upon
the text before us. He holds that the mentioning of
"the fowl of the air" between "the beast of the earth"
and "all that moveth upon the earth" is a proof that
there is a wide distinction between the physical form
of the former and all that is included in the latter.
He also holds that all the quadrupeds, domestic and
wild beasts are included in the expression "all that
moveth upon the earth." If the reader will examine
Gen. 1:28 he will readily see that the creatures
signified in the expression "all that moveth upon the
earth" are the creeping things. So the real meaning
of the text before us is this: The fear and dread of
man was to be upon every beast of the earth—that is,
all the domestic beasts and all the wild beasts—and
upon every fowl of the air, and upon all the creeping
things, and upon all the fishes of the sea. Dr. Young's
translation of this text will bear out this interpretation.
It reads as follows: "And your fear and your dread is
on every beast of the earth, and on every fowl of the
heavens, and upon all that creepeth upon the ground,
and on all the fishes of the sea; into your hand they
have been given." So the expression "all that moveth
upon the earth" can not include the quadrupeds,

either domestic or wild, because the expression has
special reference to the creeping things. The quadrupeds must therefore be included in the expression
"every beast of the earth," or they are not included
at all; and if not, then the real meaning of the text is
that the fear of man is upon all the Negroes, and upon
all the birds, and upon the reptiles, and upon the fishes;
but is not upon any of the quadrupeds. You can
readily see the lameness of Mr. Carroll's interpretation.

I will now pass to another text which our author
shamefully twists. "Bearing in mind the distinction
which God makes between the cattle or quadrupeds and
the beast or ape, the following, in common with other
punishments which God said he would inflict upon the
Israelites if they violated his law, is significant: 'And
thy carcass shall be meat unto all fowls of the air, and
unto the beasts of the earth, and no man shall fray
them away.' 'Then said David to the Philistine, . . .
This day will the Lord deliver thee into mine hand;
and I will smite thee, and take thine head from thee;
and I will give the carcases of the host of the Philistines this day unto the fowls of the air, and to the wild
beasts of the earth.' " Mr. Carroll's comment upon
this text is as follows: "This indicates that there were
wild beasts of the earth in that region in that day.
They had doubtless been emancipated. And it is

significant that every one of the great nations of that
region, with the exception of a scattered remnant of
the Israelites, are destroyed from off the earth, and
their civilizations are in ruins. . . . Thus the Bible
plainly teaches that there is a beast or ape that is a
man-eater, yet not one of the recognized apes of to-
day are man-eaters. What became of this great man-
eating ape? When we appeal to science to solve this
problem, she promptly invades the so-called human
species and points to the Negro as the highest grade of
ape, and the only ape that is a man-eater."—Pages
200, 201.

Mr. Carroll seems to be uninformed in regard to the
existence of many species of wild quadrupeds that are
carnivorous in their nature and will devour human
flesh as well as the flesh of animals. These carnivorous
quadrupeds are the beasts mentioned in this text. If
we turn to Isa. 56:9 we will find the carnivorous beasts
of the Bible lands divided into two classes, as follows:
"All ye beasts of the field, come to devour, yea, all ye
beasts in the forest." Observe that he speaks of man-
eating beasts of the field, and man-eating beasts of the
forest. According to this there must have been some
beasts of the field—which beyond doubt refers to
domestic beasts—and some beasts of the forest—which
beyond doubt refers to the wild beasts that were car-

nivorous in their nature and would sometimes devour human flesh. Let us see if we can not find an account of these two classes of carnivorous beasts in the Bible.

In Jer. 15:3 we read: "And I will appoint over them four kinds, saith the Lord: the sword to slay, and the dogs to tear, and the fowls of the heaven, and the beasts of the earth, to devour and destroy." Here the prophet also mentions two classes of carnivorous beasts. He mentions the dogs, which are domestic beasts, and some beasts beside them. Beasts in this text again is translated by the word *therion*, in the LXX., which, as before stated, signifies wild beasts. In the LXX., therefore, the text reads as follows: "And I will punish them with four kinds of death, saith the Lord, the sword to slay, and the dogs to tear, and the wild beasts of the earth, and the birds of the sky to devour and destroy." Here we have set forth very clearly the two classes of carnivorous beasts—the dogs as the domestic, and the wild beasts of the earth. Throughout the Bible these two classes of beasts are spoken of in the threats of Jehovah.

In 1 Kings 14:11 God threatens the family of Jeroboam with destruction by dogs. In 1 Kings 16:4 he threatens the family of Baasha with destruction by dogs. In 1 Kings 21:19 the prophet predicted that the dogs should lick the blood of Ahab. In the 23d

verse of the same chapter Jezebel was threatened with
destruction by dogs. The 24th verse threatens Ahab's
children with destruction by dogs. In 1 Kings 22:38
we read that dogs actually licked the blood of Ahab.
The dog was a fearful devourer in the holy lands, hence
the Psalmist sang in his hymn, "Deliver my soul from
the sword, my darling from the power of the dog."—
Ps. 22:20. The dogs are the very domestic beasts of
the field that devoured human beings in the Bible
lands.

Let us now search for the names of some of the wild
beasts of the forest that people feared in the Bible
lands. In 2 Kings 2:24 we read of two she bears that
came out of the wood and devoured forty-two children
who mocked the prophet Elisha. In 1 Kings 13:26
we read of the devouring of an untrue prophet by a
lion. In 1 Kings 20:36 a lion devoured a man who
disobeyed the word of the Lord by a prophet. In
2 Kings 17:25 we read of the devouring by lions of
some of the Gentiles whom the king of Assyria
brought to Samaria to dwell there in the place of the
Israelites whom he carried to Assyria. In Jer. 5:6 the
wolf, the lion, and the leopard are mentioned as carnivorous wild beasts by which the inhabitants of Jerusalem were threatened with destruction. It is useless
to follow this subject further. We have cited enough

scriptural evidences to give us a correct understanding
of the devouring beasts with which God threatened
to destroy the Israelites if they disobeyed him.

But it would be well to mark that in both the texts
cited by our author (Deut. 28:26; 1 Sam. 17:45, 46),
the word beast is rendered wild beasts in the LXX.
So the texts have special reference to lions, leopards,
wolves, and such like, and have no reference whatever
to the Negro; in fact, there is not a ghost of evidence
that there were any Negroes in that country to fear.

We come next to our author's twist upon Exod.
9:1-10. "Further evidence of the broad distinction
which God makes between the cattle and beast is
shown in the narrative of the plagues with which God
afflicted the Egyptians to compel them to let Israel
go. After afflicting them with frogs, lice, flies, etc.,
God said to Pharaoh, 'Let my people go, that they may
serve me. For if thou refuse to let them go, and wilt
hold them still, behold, the hand of the Lord is upon
thy cattle which is in the field, upon the horses, upon
the asses, upon the camels, upon the oxen, and upon the
sheep: there shall be a very grievous murrain. And
the Lord shall sever between the cattle of Israel and
the cattle of Egypt: and there shall nothing die of
all that is the children's of Israel. . . . And the Lord
did that thing on the morrow, and all the cattle of

Egypt died: but of the cattle of the children of Israel died not one. . . . And the heart of Pharaoh was hardened, and he did not let the people go. And the Lord said unto Moses and unto Aaron, Take to you handfuls of ashes of the furnace, and let Moses sprinkle it toward the heaven in the sight of Pharaoh. And it shall become small dust in all the land of Egypt, and shall be a boil breaking forth with blains upon man, and upon beast, throughout all the land of Egypt. And they took ashes of the furnace, and stood before Pharaoh; and Moses sprinkled it up toward heaven; and it became a boil breaking forth with blains upon man, and upon beast.'

"We are thus taught that the cattle are quadrupeds, horses camels, etc., and that the beasts were a very different class of animals, as shown by the fact that the cattle were first afflicted, then afterwards the beasts were afflicted. This is significant when we consider that each succeeding plague was more injurious to the Egyptians than its predecessor. This indicates the relative value of the cattle and beasts, and that the beasts were far more valuable than the cattle. We can readily understand that this would be so when we realize that the cattle were their domestic quadrupeds and their beasts were Negroes."—Pages 203-205.

Mr. Carroll, like scripture-twisters generally, does not read far enough to get a correct understanding of the Bible. Had he read just a few verses further in the chapter from which he quotes he would have seen that his theory is all a heresy. The very next plague that was sent upon the Egyptians explains perfectly the significations of the words cattle and beast as used in the record of the plagues. It was the plague of hail. It was predicted by Moses unto Pharaoh in the following words: "Behold, to-morrow about this time I will cause it to rain a very grievous hail, such as hath not been in Egypt since the foundation thereof even until now. Send therefore now, and gather thy cattle, and all that thou hast in the field; for upon every man and beast which shall be found in the field, and shall not be brought home, the hail shall come down upon them, and they shall die."— Verses 18, 19.

This is not correct language if the words beast and cattle are not significant of exactly the same thing. But let us see how the Egyptians understood this prophecy. "He that feared the word of the Lord among the servants of Pharaoh made his servants and his cattle flee into the houses: and he that regarded not the word of the Lord left his servants and his cattle in the field." —Verses 20, 21. Observe that there were two classes in the field that were in danger—servants and cattle. The plague was to injure man and beast. If, therefore, we accept Mr. Carroll's theory, that the beasts were the Negroes, we must believe that the men were the cattle, because the plague was to injure man and beast and in the field there were servants and cattle. Surely he has peculiar names for some things. Would it not be more sensible to accept the facts so plainly set forth here, that the cattle were the beasts, and the servants were the men?

We here confront Mr. Carroll also with another astounding argument. If the Egyptians at that time possessed Negroes, as he states, and owned and worked them as servants, this text then certainly calls the Negroes men; and he can not dodge the fact. The plague of the boils and the plague of the hail came upon the same creatures. The boils came upon men and beasts, or cattle; and the plague of the hail came upon men and the beasts, or cattle. It is not difficult to place a sensible interpretation upon these texts that destroys all the proofs our author sees in them, that the Negro is a beast.

I will now take up another of our author's twists. He sets it forth as follows: "The Canaanites whom the Israelites were commanded to destroy and possess themselves of their country were the owners of great numbers of Negroes, as shown by the following: 'And the Lord thy God will put out those nations before, thee by little and little: thon mayest not consume them at once, lest the beasts of the field increase upon thee.'—Deut. 7:22. Observe that there was no fear expressed lest the cattle or the creeping thing increased upon the Israelites; but not so with the beasts of the field, or Negroes. Let us bear in mind that the country of the Canaanites was a rich productive country, a goodly land, and that it was in the highest state of cultivation. . . . It was occupied by seven nations greater and mightier than Israel, and it would have been impossible for this comparatively small number of Israelites to have occupied the numerous fine cities, towns, villages, farms, etc., and maintain this splendid civilization which had required ages to develop. . . . Hence it was the part of wisdom for the Israelites to first possess themselves of only so much of the land as they could successfully handle, leaving the remainder, with its wealth and civilization, in the hands of the Canaanites to care for and preserve. . . . The Negro is as prolific as the white and would increase as rapidly. They would prove very troublesome neighbors, as the free Negro never fails to prove."— Pages 206, 207.

Is it possible that our author knows of no living

creatures among the lower animals that inhabited the land of Canaan besides creeping things and cattle? Is it possible that he does not know how numerous and troublesome dogs were in that rich land at that time? Also is it possible that he does not know how mean and troublesome the foxes were? Does he know nothing about the bears and lions, and the many other wild species of animals of that country, that would traverse the fields of Canaan as well as the forest? These are the animals that Jehovah feared would increase upon the Israelites, not the Negroes. This text is no proof that the Canaanites possessed Negroes. It simply expresses the fear that the beasts of the field would increase too fast and become troublesome to the Israelites. In the LXX. this text calls the beasts "wild beasts" of the field. This confirms our interpretation.

We now come to another of Mr. Carroll's twists. "The evidence that the Israelites possessed Negroes is found in the following command: 'Six years thou shalt sow thy land, and shalt gather in the fruits thereof: but the seventh year thou shalt let it rest and lie still; that the poor of thy people may eat: and what they leave the beasts of the field shall eat. In like manner thou shalt deal with thy vineyard, and with thy olive-yard.' Here we have additional and positive proof that the beast of the field is not our domestic quadrupeds of draft and burden: these animals will not eat grapes and olives." Certainly, Mr. Carroll, we would not suppose that it was the domestic beasts that are referred to here as the beast of the field, although this expression often designates them. But since there were other beasts that traversed the fields of the Israelites, that would eat these fruits, we can at a glance see the application of this term; for instance, the fox. We know that from time immemorial he has been an enemy to grapes, and is spoken of as such throughout the Bible: and they must have been very numerous in that country, because Sampson when he wished to inflict a severe punishment upon the Philistines caught three hundred foxes and tied firebrands to their tails and turned them loose, which resulted in the destruction of the grain fields of the Philistines. They must have been as numerous in that country as the ground squirrels are to-day in the state of Washington, or the jack-rabbits in California. I think they, with what help they would get from some other species of small animals that traversed their fields, could take care of all the fruit in the Sabbatical year that the travelers left. So we can see no Negroes in this text either.

I will now take up our author's idea of the serpent

that beguiled Eve. After quoting the narrative of the
fall in the third chapter of Genesis, he says: "We
observe (1) that the tempter of Eve was a beast of the
field. This would scarcely have been more clearly
indicated had the text read, Now the serpent was more
subtle than any other beast of the field which the
Lord God had made. (2) It is evident that when
Adam gave names to every beast of the field with which
he was associated in the garden of Eden, in his efforts
to dress it and keep it, the characteristics displayed by
this individual led Adam to name it the serpent. This
was simply a name given it to distinguish it from
others of its kind. Hence the name serpent no more
indicates that it was a snake than does the name of the
late Indian Chief, Sitting Bull, indicate that he is a
bull which habitually assumed the sitting posture. . . .

"The modern clergy teach that the first sin which
Adam and Eve committed was their eating of the forbidden fruit. This, as shown by the record, is in
direct conflict with the plain teaching of the Bible.
When they accepted as their counselor this creature
over which they were designed to have dominion,
they violated those original statutes given man in the
creation, and thus brought sin into the world. Instead
of controlling this beast of the field, or Negro—the
serpent—they allowed him to control them, and he led

them to their ruin. . . . We observe that the first
curses which God visited upon the serpent were directed
solely at its posture. Had the tempter of Eve been a
snake, God's sentence 'Upon thy belly shalt thou go'
would have been of no effect. It would not have
wrought the slightest change in the posture of the
snake, neither would it have occasioned him the least
inconvenience. On the other hand, it would have
placed God in the most ridiculous light, since the only
way the snake could go was upon its belly. But when
we come to understand that the tempter of Eve was a
beast—a Negro—the whole subject appears in a very
different light. The habitual posture of the Negro is
the erect; hence God's sentence, 'Upon thy belly shalt
thou go,' wrought the most radical change in this
Negro's posture, and was a most terrible punishment.
When God cursed him above every beast of the field it
deprived him of his erect posture. · When God cursed
him above all cattle he was prevented from going on
all fours like the quadrupeds. 'Upon thy belly shalt
thou go' degraded him in point of posture to the level
of the lowest creeping things. God's other curse
upon the serpent, 'I will put enmity between thee and
the woman, and between thy seed and her seed: it
shall bruise thy head, and thou shalt bruise his heel,'
shows that the tempter of Eve was a material creature,

a creature of flesh and blood, and that he begat offspring; and it is highly probable that he was the parent
of Cain's paramour of strange flesh, and that this curse
was fufilled in Cain's ultimate banishment from the
Adamic family, to become a fugitive and a vagabond
in the earth, and an outcast in eternity. It should be
necessary to state that God's curses upon the tempter
of Eve were confined to this individual beast, and did
not extend to the rest of the Negroes, since they were
not parties to his crime."—Pages 217-220.

It is remarkable how our author can make almost
any word mean Negro. He can not only change the
word beast into Negro, but he can take also the word
serpent, that has had a fixed definition among men for
many thousand years, and change it so that it no
longer means a reptile, but a black biped beast, or
Negro. I am sure if this theory were true, the poor
Negro that tempted Adam and Eve deserved the
sympathy of all men of that day, especially of his son-
in-law (?) Cain. To creep upon his belly as long as he
lived would certainly have made that part of his body
very sore by times, especially when he would traverse
earth that had a sprinkling of gravel in it! But I
wonder how God made him creep? Did he clip off
his arms and legs? Surely not; for without them he
could not have crept. He could not twist his body

like a snake, and thus move himself over the ground.
He needed his arms and legs to help propel his body.
Well, if God left his hands and legs upon his body,
how could he make him creep? not by taking physical
strength out of him; for it would require greater
physical strength for a creature of the form of a Negro
to push his body along in a creeping manner than it
would to walk on all fours or upright. This is surely
a puzzling question. I wish Mr. Carroll had attempted
to explain it. Well, I must say that his theory here
is ridiculous in the extreme. If we let the Bible alone
and and let it mean what it says, we always have a
sensible interpretation of its teachings; but when we
change men into beasts and snakes into men, we
always are confronted with ridiculous and conflicting
ideas.

Mr. Carroll seems to think that the classifying of
the serpent among the beasts of the field, is proof
that he was no snake. Well, I am sure it is no proof
to me that he was not a snake; because snakes are
called beasts in the Bible, even in the New Testament.
We read in the twenty-eighth chapter of Acts and third
verse that Paul in the island of Melita was bitten by a
viper, and this viper fastened on his hand. The next
verse says, "And when the barbarians saw the veno-
mous beast hang on his hand," etc.; then in the fifth

verse we read of Paul, "And he shook off the beast into the fire, and felt no harm." In this place a snake is evidently called a beast. So if snakes were called beasts in Paul's day, it is perfectly reasonable to suppose that they were considered beasts in the time of Moses, who handed down to us the history of the fall as we have it in the third chapter of Genesis. The word serpent signifies a species of snake, and why not let the word alone and conclude that it means what it has always been understood to mean? The apostle Paul, when speaking of the fall of our first parents, says, "The serpent beguiled Eve through his subtlety." Why (if Mr. Carroll's position be right) did Paul not correct the misunderstanding of the people of his day by telling the Corinthians plainly that it was a Negro that tempted Eve? Why should he have used a word that the entire Greek world understood to signify a snake? I am sure that every ray of evidence substantiates the belief that the beguiling serpent was a serpent; not an ape, nor a Negro, nor a white man, nor a brown, yellow, or red man. He was simply a snake; and the very record of Genesis 3 itself proves it.

How then possessed he the ability to speak? some may say. It is easy enough to explain that. The spirit of old Beelzebub was in him, and *he* can talk through anything. Devils spoke when Christ was upon earth, on several occasions; others beside Jesus heard their voices when he was casting evil spirits out of certain human beings. To-day the devil speaks through many human beings who are consecrated to carry his false and delusive doctrines to the ends of the earth. Hence the devil no longer speaks through snakes. But at the time our first parents were beguiled there were only two human beings upon earth, Adam and Eve, and they were both holy. The devil could not get possession of either of them; hence he must look for the very wisest of the creatures among the lower animals, and he surely made a wise choice; for the Son of God himself sets the serpent up as an example of wisdom, and tells his humble followers to be "wise as serpents." So the devil was compelled to condescend to call the serpent to be his first preacher; and having made choice of him, he could, and did, talk through that snake. From this time the poor snake was made to creep on his belly all the days of his life.

But Mr. Carroll would ask, How could God punish him by making him creep, when he was already a creeper? This could very easily have been done. The snake might have possessed legs, like the lizard, before this time; and surely he did. The lizard is *properly* classed among the creepers, yet he does not

creep on his belly like the snake.   Would it not be a
perfectly reasonable theory that the snake before the
fall possessed legs, like the lizard or ground-puppy,
and that as a punishment for the service he rendered
to the devil in overthrowing our first parents God
clipped his legs off, and caused him ever since to creep
upon his belly as he does to-day?   God could do this
as easily as he could make legs grow upon a tadpole,
and at the same time cause his tail to drop off, and
convert him into a frog.   If we let the word serpent
alone and let it mean snake, we can easily understand
the other part of the curse placed upon the snake;
namely, "I will put enmity between thee and the
woman, and between thy seed and her seed: it shall
bruise thy head, and thou shalt bruise his heel."   That
very enmity exists between snakes and women to-day.
There is nothing so fearful for a woman to look upon
as a snake.   The enmity also exists between all the
woman's seed and the snake's seed.   The first thing
thought of by a man or boy on beholding a snake is to
provide himself with a club with which to bruise his
head; and, on the other hand, the snake is continually
watching his chance to bruise the boy's heel with a
severe bite.   So it is evident that we need not twist
the Bible at all to bring out its interpretation. . What
it says is the most sensible meaning that can be
attached to it.

I will now consider a very peculiar twist of our author upon Ezek. 23:20, concerning which he says: "God charges that the people of Jerusalem and Samaria committed fornication with the Egyptians, Assyrians, etc., 'whose flesh is as the flesh of asses, and whose issue is like the issue of horses.' When we turn upon this statement the light of Paul's declaration, 'There is one kind of flesh of men, another flesh of beasts,' etc., it becomes plain that the horse, the ass, and the Negro all belong to one kind of flesh—the flesh of beasts—and that the Egyptians, Assyrians, etc., had descended to amalgamation, hence their flesh was corrupted, and was strange flesh to that of the people of Jerusalem and Samaria."

These words are sufficient to prove that Mr. Carroll has not grasped the true meaning of the text before us. It has no reference to amalgamation of the literal flesh of Israel and Judah with that of the Egyptians, Assyrians, etc., but is significative of the leagues that Jerusalem and Samaria made from time to time with the Gentile nations, which caused their religion to become commingled with that of the heathen nations. This the reader can readily perceive if he reads the entire chapter, in which the prophet sets forth Jerusalem and Samaria as two daughters of one mother. He names Samaria, Aholah; that is, his tabernacle: and Jerusalem, Aholibah; that is, my tabernacle in her. It shows how these two sisters committed spiritual whoredom by making leagues with the nations about them. There is no hint at literal whoredom between individuals. The prophet calls Assyria, Samaria's lover, and states that God gave her over into the hands of her lover; which was fulfilled when the Assyrians carried away the ten tribes. Then he proceeds to show how Jerusalem failed to take warning from the fate of Samaria, and continued to fall in love with the nations about her,— especially Babylon—and that God, because she doted upon Babylon, gave her into the hands of her lover, Babylon; which was fulfilled when the Babylonians carried Judah into captivity. Speaking of these lovers,—of these unfaithful sisters—Judah and Israel, the prophet says in the text before us, "Whose flesh is as the flesh of asses, and whose issue is like the issue of horses." By this he meant to say that the Gentile nations, Babylon, Assyria, Egypt, etc., were as far from being fit companions for Judah and Israel as the ass and the horse are for a human being. There are no such thoughts contained in this text as Mr. Carroll attempts to bring out of it. There is no hint that either of the nations mentioned here had descended to amalgamation with some sort of beast and were hence composed of mixed-bloods and void of the full-blooded condition.

We now come to Mr. Carroll's twist upon the book of Jonah. He quotes from the third chapter the following words: " 'And the word of the Lord came unto Jonah the second time, saying, Arise, go into Nineveh, that great city, and preach unto it the preaching that I bid thee. So Jonah arose, and went into Nineveh, according to the word of the Lord. . . . And Jonah began to enter into the city a day's journey, and he cried, and said, Yet forty days, and Nineveh shall be overthrown. So the people of Nineveh believed God, and proclaimed a fast, and put on sackcloth, from the greatest of them even unto the least of them. For word came unto the king of Nineveh, and he arose from his throne, and he laid his robe from him, and covered him with sackcloth, and sat in ashes. And he caused it to be proclaimed and published through Nineveh by the decree of the king and his nobles, saying, Let neither man nor beast, herd nor flock, taste anything: let them not feed, nor drink water: but let man and beast be covered with sackcloth, and cry mightily unto God: yea, let them turn every one from his evil way, and from the violence that is in their hands. Who can tell if God will turn and repent, and turn away from his fierce anger, that we perish not?' "

Upon this text our author comments as follows: "We observe (1) the broad distinction made between

the herds and flocks (cattle) and the beast; (2) that
Jonah never charged the people of Nineveh with any
offences whatever: he simply proclaimed the judgment
of God, that in forty days Nineveh should be overthrown; (3) the king never questioned the authority
of Jonah, neither did he doubt the power of God who
sent him; (4) the king expressed no surprise at this
threatened visitation of God's wrath, made no inquiry
as to the cause of the trouble, nor offered any protest
against the judgment of God: on the contrary, he
fully realized the nature of the trouble and the justice
of God's judgment, by proceeding to rectify the evil
things; he issued his edict that all business should be
suspended, even to the feeding and watering of the
herds and flocks, and that all the energies of man and
beast should be concentrated to appease divine wrath,
and thus save the city; (5) the king fully realized that
it was the criminal relations existing between the men
of Nineveh and their beasts that had brought the city
to the verge of destruction under divine judgment.
This is demonstrated by the fact that he laid identically the same penalty upon man and beast. Each was
required to observe the fast, each was to be covered
with sackcloth, each must cry mightily unto God, each
must turn from his evil way and from the violence
that is in his hand. Thus it is shown that the beasts

were compelled to do identically the same things which the men of Nineveh did in their efforts to appease the wrath of God and save the city. "And God saw their works, that they turned from their evil way; and God repented of the evil, that he had said he would do unto them; and he did it not.'—Jonah 3:10."

In this place our author betrays the grossest ignorance of the language of the Bible. The language is clear enough to one who reads the Bible only to learn the true mind of the spirit that is contained in its words. We are not to understand that the beasts at Nineveh offered formal prayers to God the same as the men, but the king commanded that they should be clothed with sackcloth, and should be caused to fast the same as the men, believing that the lowing of the hungry ox, the bleating of the hungry sheep, and the neighing of the hungry horse, would call out the sympathy of God for the city. This is the sense in which the beasts cried unto God while the men were intelligently praying for mercy.

If we read the proclamation of the king of Nineveh from the LXX., we find it leaves the word beast out entirely. It is as follows: "Let not men, or cattle, or oxen, or sheep, taste anything, nor feed, nor drink water." In the next verse the LXX. states: "So men and cattle were clothed with sackcloths, and

cried earnestly to God." Surely the translators of
the LXX. in their day did not understand that the
beasts at Nineveh were black bipeds, for no such idea
comes from their translation. They even dropped out
entirely the word beast and substituted for it the word
cattle, which applies to domestic animals in general.

The king of Nineveh did not intend that his subjects should understand that some of their beasts had
hands and were guilty of sins like the men. His command, "Let them turn every one from his evil way,
and from the violence that is in their hands," they
understood well enough. The men of Nineveh know
they were the guilty parties. They repented according
to the king's commandment and the city was spared.
The fasting and crying of the beasts for food and
drink cut no figure with God. The city would have
been saved just the same upon the humility and repentance of the men of Nineveh, and the command of the
king to cause the cattle to participate in this fast is
the outgrowth of the superstition of his day.

CAIN'S WIFE AND CHILDREN.

OUR author has some strange ideas about Cain's wife and children. He thinks that no daughters were born unto Adam and Eve prior to the time referred to in the text which says, "And Cain knew his wife, and she conceived, and bare Enoch."—Gen. 4:17. I should like very much to know how he found out that Adam and Eve had no daughters prior to this time. The Bible does not say they did not have, and there is not a straw of evidence anywhere that they did not have daughters prior to this time. How then can our author be so positive as to say emphatically as he does on page 152 of his book: "There were no daughters born to Adam until after the birth of Seth"? Gen. 5:4, which states that the days of Adam after he had begotten Seth were eight hundred years, and he begat sons and daughters, is no proof that he had not begotten daughters prior to the birth of Seth. Adam was, at the time of Seth's birth, according to the received chronology, one hundred thirty years old; according to the chronology of the LXX., two hundred thirty years old.

To say that Adam and Eve kept house all this time
and were only the parents of three children, when their
eldest had been born unto them so soon after their
creation, is the grossest kind of assumption. They
surely up till that time had begotten a great number
of children. But whether they had begotten few or
many daughters, we know that they had at least begotten one, because Cain possessed a wife at the time of
his banishment, and there was no living creature upon
earth capable of being a wife unto Cain except one of
the daughters of Eve; because in Gen. 3:20 we read:
"And Adam called his wife's name Eve [that is, *life*],
because she was the mother of all living." This is a
proof that there was no source from which Cain could
have obtained a wife except from among the daughters
of Eve.

Our author puts forth a peculiar twist upon the
record of the offering up of sacrifices unto God by Cain
and Abel in Gen. 4. The inspired record is as follows:
"And in process of time it came to pass, that Cain
brought of the fruit of the ground an offering unto the
Lord. And Abel, he also brought of the firstlings of
his flock, and of the fat thereof. And the Lord had
respect unto Abel, and to his offering: but unto Cain
and to his offering he had not respect. And Cain was
very wroth, and his countenance fell. And the Lord

said unto Cain, Why art thou wroth? and why is thy
countenance fallen? If thou doest well, shalt thou not
be accepted? and if thou doest not well, sin lieth at the
door. And unto thee shall be his desire, and thou
shalt rule over him. And Cain talked with Abel his
brother: and it came to pass, when they were in the
field, that Cain rose up against Abel his brother, and
slew him."—Gen. 4:3-8.

Our author thinks that the sin which caused Cain's
offering to be rejected by God was amalgamation with
a Negress, and he seems to see in the inspired record
that Cain had an associate in his sin. After quoting
from Gen. 4:7, "Unto thee shall be his desire, and
thou shalt rule over him," he comments as follows:
"This indicates that Cain had not only violated the
law of God, but that he had an associate in the crime.
To have desire requires life, and also requires intelli-
gence. No inanimate object can have desire. In view
of the fact that individuals of the same sex have no
desire for each other, it would seem natural to decide
that this creature which had desire for this fine young
man Cain was a female; and the mere fact that the
inspired writer refers to it in the masculine gender is
not evidence that it was not a female."—Page 141.

Here again our author has committed a great error
by not grasping the meaning of scripture. It is

strange that he would come short of the correct understanding of a text that is so plain as this.   I am sure
there is no hint at any accomplice in Cain's sins, in
this record, to one whose mind is not biased by a false
theory.   The words, "His desire shall be unto thee, and
thou shalt rule over him," contain a prophecy of
Jehovah concerning the murder of Abel by Cain, which
the record tells us soon afterwards occurred.   In this
Cain actually did rule over his brother and subdue him,
even to the destruction of his life.   This can have no
reference whatever to Cain's wife.   The word desire,
which our author thinks is evidence that the masculine
referred to was a female, is not contained in the text in
the LXX., which reads as follows: "Be still; to thee
shall be his submission, and thou shalt rule over him." ·
This rendering is very clear and does away entirely
with Mr. Carroll's theory.

The sin which caused Jehovah to reject Cain's
sacrifice was not amalgamation with a beast.   There
are good reasons for believing that it was a wrong
committed by him in the manner in which he offered
his sacrifice.   Paul tells us in Heb. 11:4, "By faith
Abel offered unto God a more excellent sacrifice than
Cain."   So Cain's sin was unbelief, as the Apostle
Paul understood it; and I am sure that I would prefer
his teaching as an inspired apostle to that of Mr. Car-

roll, who styles himself "The Revelator of the Century."

I would state further, that there is no evidence that Cain possessed a wife prior to the time he and Abel came together to worship God, although he may have possessed one prior to this time But the first record we have of Cain's wife, was speaking of him after he had been banished to the land of Nod subsequent to the murder of his brother Abel.

Mr. Carroll thinks he sees a proof in the epistle of Jude that Cain's wife was a Negress. Verse 11 of said epistle reads as follows: "Woe unto them! for they have gone in the way of Cain, and ran greedily after the error of Balaam for reward, and perished in the gainsaying of Core." Mr. Carroll tries to tie this verse in a peculiar manner to the seventh verse, which speaks of Sodom and Gomorrah giving themselves over to fornication and going after strange flesh, and tries to make it appear that both verses apply to the same class of people, and that the fornication and going after strange flesh in the seventh verse is the going in the way of Cain mentioned in the eleventh verse. But this is only another of his twists. It is easy to understand by the reading of this epistle that there are two classes of people referred to in these two verses. The seventh verse has special reference to Sodom and

Gomorrah and the cities about them, and the eleventh verse has special reference to a class of people who lived in the time of Jude, whom Jude says in verse 12 were spots in the Christians' feast of charity. Mr. Carroll, by tying these two verses together and applying them to one class of people, as above mentioned, and then advocating the idea that fornication and going after strange flesh signifies amalgamation with the Negroes, seems to think he has a strong proof that Cain's sin for which he was banished to the land of Nod and made a fugitive and a vagabond all the days of his life, was amalgamation with a Negro. Ridiculous nonsense! There is no idea of amalgamation with a Negro in the word fornication, neither is there any idea of amalgamation in the expression "going after strange flesh," which was one of the sins of the Sodomites. This expression doubtless refers to the filthy practice of sexual congress with beasts, such as Moses forbade in the 18th chapter of Leviticus. But the fact that they condescended to this degrading sin is no proof of amalgamation, since there is no hint at an offspring produced thereby.

The sins of the people of his own day Jude divides into three classes in verse 11. (1) Going in the way of Cain; (2) running greedily after the error of Balaam; (3) perished in the gainsaying of Core. The Bible explains all these sins. The way of Cain was that of murder; for the Bible tells us that he was the first murderer. For his crime he was banished to the land of Nod and made a fugitive all the days of his life.

The error of Balaam is that of whoredom. It is called the casting of a stumbling-block before Israel in Rev. 2:14. Balaam was a prophet of God in the time of Israel's exodus from Egypt. He was sent for by king Balak to curse the Israelites. Balaam, after earnest pleadings from Balak, went to Balak to offer several sacrifices unto God, but each time a blessing came from God upon Israel instead of a curse, which greatly enraged king Balak against the prophet Balaam. Balaam, then, to appease the king's wrath, taught him to send out a great many women toward the camps of the Israelites, to entice the men of Israel to commit whoredom with them. Balaam told Balak that if he succeeded in this, God would curse Israel because of this great sin. Balak followed the instructions of Balaam and in this way succeeded in bringing down a curse from heaven upon the Israelites. For an account of this stumbling-block of Balaam, see Numbers, chapters 22-25. .

The stumbling-block which Balaam taught Balak to cast before Israel is described by Philo Judæus, a writer who lived contemporary with Josephus, as

follows: "O king, the women of the country surpass
all other women in beauty, and there are no means by
which a man is more easily subdued than by the
beauty of a woman. Therefore if you enjoin the most
beautiful of them to grant their favors to them and to
prostitute themselves before them, they will allure and
overcome the youth of your enemies. But you must
warn them not to surrender their beauty to those who
desire them with too great facility and too speedily,
for resistance and coyness will stimulate the passions
and excite them more, and will kindle a more impet-
uous desire; and so being wholly subdued by their
appetites they will endure to do and to suffer anything.
And let any damsel who is thus prepared for the sport
resist and say wantonly to a lover who is thus influenced,
It is not fit for you to enjoy my society until you have
first abandoned your native habits and have changed
and learned to honor the same practice that I do, and
I must have a conspicuous proof of your real change,
which I can only have by your consenting to join me
in the same sacrifices and libations which I use and
which we may then offer together to the same images
and statues and other erections in honor of my gods.
And the lover being as it were taken in the net of her
manifold and multiform snares, not being able to resist
her beauty and seductive conversation, will become

wholly subdued in his reason and, like a miserable man, will obey all the commands which she lays upon him, and will be enrolled as the slave of passion."—From Philo's Life of Moses, Book 1, Par. 54. According to this account of Philo the error of Balaam included idolatry with whoredom.

"The gainsaying of Core" was a rebellion raised against Moses by Korah, Dathan, and Abiram, for which they and their companies perished. The earth opened her mouth and swallowed up them and their companies, and they went down alive into hades. So there is no amalgamation with Negroes mentioned by the apostle Jude. He simply denounces the wicked people of his time for the sin of murder, adultery, idolatry, and rebellion against God.

Let us now take a look at Cain's children from Carroll's standpoint of viewing things. Concerning them he says on page 150 of his book: "Cain's wife being a Negress, it follows that her offspring by Cain were mixed-bloods. This explains why Cain and his descendants were thrust out of the line of descent from Adam to the Savior. Cain was the sole representative of the Adamic creation of his family; hence the only living soul. The last vestige of immortality in his family disappeared when the spirit of Cain, whose crimes of murder and amalgamation made him a fugitive and a vagabond, in time took its flight from earth to receive the doom of the outcast in eternity.''

The reader will understand our author in this place better when I shall have shown in a succeeding chapter that he teaches that mixed-bloods have no souls. He holds that the Negro, whom he styles a beast, is composed only of mind and matter; and that the Caucasian, who only he styles man, is composed of mind, matter, and soul; and that a mixture produced between them is only mind and matter like the Negro, hence not human. So we are to understand him to teach in this place that the children of Cain were not human beings; that is, neither men and women, nor male and female beasts, but a new species produced by a cross between man and beast. Mark that he states emphatically that Cain was the only immortal soul in his family. He means by this that his wife was a beast, and therefore possessed no soul, and that his children were mixed-bloods—neither man nor beast—and hence possessed no souls.

As we follow our author further in his story, we find him speaking concerning the sons of God who fell in love with and married the daughters of men (Gen. 6:2), as follows: "The sons of God were the white males who traced their pedigree through a line of pure-blooded ancestors to Adam, and the daughters of men were mixed-blooded females who traced their pedigree to men on the paternal side and to Negroes on the maternal side. Their fathers were men, but their mothers were Negroes—apes, beasts—hence the unions of the male descendants of Adam and these mixed-blooded females resulted in further corrupting the earth, and finally led God in his wrath and disgust to destroy them with the deluge."—Page 153.

Our author has placed himself in a dilemma here. If, as he states, these sons of God were pure-blooded children of Adam and the daughters of men were half men and half beast and, according to his doctrine, had no souls, and were not human, the children of these marriages would, like their mothers, have been only beasts, and not men; but right here the Bible comes in with a stunning rebuke against this false theory, when it says concerning the children that were born to the sons of God by the daughters of men: "When the sons of God came in unto the daughters of men, and they bare children to them, the same became mighty *men* which were of old, MEN of renown."— Gen. 6:4. I would like to have our author explain to us how he is going to dispose of this text that so flatly contradicts his theory.

He teaches concerning mixed-bloods, on page 129 of his book, as follows: "But, says the enlightened Christian, If a man is married to a Negress, will not their offspring have a soul? No. It is simply the product resulting from God's violated law and inherits none of the divine nature of man; but, like its parent, the ape, it is merely a combination of matter and mind. Then if a half-breed marries a man, will not their offspring have a soul? No. Then if a three-quarter white marries a man, will not their offspring have a soul? No. If the offspring of man and the Negro are mated with pure whites for generations, will not their ultimate offspring have a soul? No."

We can not misunderstand our author here. He plainly gives us to understand that if a creature has one drop of Negro blood in him he has no soul; hence is not a man. Then he tells us one thing concerning the children of God by the daughters of men, and the Bible tells us another. He makes out that they are not men, and the Bible says they were "mighty *men; MEN* of renown." "Let God be true, but every man a liar."—Rom. 3:4.

Following our author still further in his story, we find him taking up the Bible account of Noah as follows: "But just at this critical juncture, the most critical that man has ever known, when the nature of Almighty God was aroused in his just wrath to destroy from the earth, which their shameless crime had cor-

THESE ARE NOT MEN—HAVE NO SOULS.—*Carroll.*
THEY ARE MIGHTY MEN—MEN OF RENOWN.—*Gen. 6:4*

rupted, the last vestige of the seed of man, Noah found grace in the eyes of the Lord (Gen. 6:8). Why? 'Noah was a just man, and perfect in his generations, and Noah walked with God.'—Gen. 6:9. It will be observed that there are three characteristics here recorded of Noah which are assigned as so many reasons why Noah found grace in the eyes of the Lord. (1) Noah was a just man. (2) He was perfect in his generations. (3) Noah walked with God. . . . This characteristic in Noah, that he was perfect in his generations, was not the result of any act upon his part, and all credit for his possession of it is due solely to his ancestors, who transmitted to him from Adam in uncorrupted line of descent the pure Adamic stock."—Pages 154, 155.

Here again our author fails to grasp the meaning of the sacred scriptures. The expression, "perfect in *his* generations" has no reference whatever to any of the generations that preceeded Noah, but to the generation living upon earth in the time of Noah. The plurality of the word generation proves nothing to the contrary of what we are here stating. We can not always found a great argument upon the number of a word in a dead language. In the LXX. this word occurs in the singular. In it the text reads: "Noah was a just man, perfect in his generation; Noah was well-pleasing to God."—This must be the correct rendering, because the perfection of Noah is referred to again in Gen. 7:1, where the word generation occurs in the singular. "And the Lord God said unto Noah, Come thou and all thy house into the ark; for thee have I seen righteous before me in this generation." This explains the perfection of Noah. It was a moral perfection before the generation living upon the earth in his time; and the Scriptures do not intend to base Noah's perfection upon anything transmitted to him through his ancestors. It might be well to observe also that the word perfect i. the expression, "perfect in his generations," is rendered upright in the margin of our Bible. This throws the text in perfect harmony with Gen. 7:1. Translating the word perfect by the word upright, as in the margin, and the word generations in the singular, as in the LXX., the two texts will read thus: "Noah was a just man and upright in his generation."—Gen. 6:9. "Thee have I seen righteous before me in this generation."—Gen. 7:1. It seems to me that any Bible student ought to readily comprehend the nature of Noah's perfection, and that it has no reference to the nature of the stock of humanity of which he was bred, but to the uprightness of his heart and life before God and the people of his day.

CARROLL'S THEORY OF AMALGAMATION.

M<small>R.</small> C<small>ARROLL'S</small> entire theory might be summed up as follows: God in the beginning created man male and female, and man was white. Prior to the creation of man he created a beast male and female, and the beast was black, and the beast was created to work for man, and man was to do the planning and bossing. And it came to pass that the sons of men lusted after the daughters of the black beasts and took of them unto themselves for wives. And it came to pass that children were born unto the men who had married beasts, and their children were neither black nor white, but some were yellow, and some were brown, and some were red. And it came to pass that God was exasperated at this wickedness of men, and he sent a great flood of waters to destroy them. But luckily for us, he found one man who had no beast blood in him, whom he preserved with his family. But unluckily for the people of this age, he preserved also from destruction by that flood a pair of the black beasts. *And it* came to pass again when men were multiplied upon the earth that they lusted after the female beasts and took of them unto themselves for wives, and children were born unto them, who, like the children of those who had sinned in like manner before the flood, were neither white nor black, but some were red, and some were brown, and some were yellow. And these children of men by the black female beasts possessed no souls. And it came to pass by and by that the Messiah came to destroy this sin of amalgamation, but his influence was soon overcome by the apostasy and amalgamation went on as before, until it entirely destroyed the church of Christ; and to-day the professed church of Christ is making a fool of itself in trying to teach these soulless mixed-blooded apes the way of life and bring them to Christ.

I have proven our author's theory false in regard to the creation of the black beast. I have also proven that his theory of amalgamation before the flood is unscriptural. In this chapter I desire to take up the nature of his doctrine of amalgamation and show that it is a thing impossible, and neither scriptural nor philosophical, after which I will follow him in the consideration of a number of texts which he twists in his efforts to prove that the sin of amalgamation has been visited by the judgments of God upon men of various nations in various ages.

In several places in his book he makes use of Paul's words in 1 Cor. 15:39. "All flesh is not the same flesh, but there is one kind of flesh of men, another flesh of beasts, another of fishes, and another of birds." He endeavors to show that the Negro is an ape, and hence his flesh belongs to that class of flesh which Paul styles the flesh of beasts. But he does not proceed far with his theory before he meets a most stubborn obstacle; namely, the Negro will breed true to the human family. He tries to dodge this obstacle in a desperate floundering effort to prove that there is a beast mentioned in the Bible with which men may have connection and produce offspring. He quotes Lev. 18:23, which reads as follows: "Neither shalt thou lie with any beast to defile thyself therewith: neither shall any woman stand before a beast to lie down thereto; it is confusion." Also he quotes Lev. 20:15, 16, which says: "And if a man lie with a beast, he shall surely be put to death: and ye shall slay the beast. And if a woman approach unto any beast, and lie down thereto, thou shalt kill the woman, and the beast: they shall surely be put to death; their blood shall be upon them."

Commenting upon the first of these texts he says: "Confusion, mixing, mingling are synonymous terms; *hence* there should be no mixing, no mingling, no

confusion of man's blood with that of a beast." Commenting upon the second of these texts he says: "Thus
the immediate offspring of man and the Negro—the
mulatto—was doomed by divine edict to instant death
in the very moment of conception; hence neither the
mulatto nor his ultimate offspring can acquire a right
to live. This being true it follows that these monstrosities have no rights, social, financial, political, or
religious that men need respect. They have no rights
that men dare respect, not even the right to live."

There are no such things taught in these texts as
our author tries to bring out of them. They truly
show the possibility of intercourse between man and
beast, but they produce not an iota of evidence that
this connection will produce offspring. There is no
mention of such offspring in these texts or anywhere
else in the Bible. The little clause, "it is confusion,"
applied to the intercourse of man with beast does not
prove the production of offspring. If so, what can be
the meaning of the same clause applied to the intercourse of man with his daughter-in-law, in Lev. 20:12,
which says, "If a man lie with his daughter-in-law,
both of them shall surely be put to death: they have
wrought confusion"? If the word confusion in Lev.
18:23 proves mixed-blooded offspring, as Mr. Carroll
states, the same word in Lev. 20:12 also proves mixed-

blooded offspring. But Mr. Carroll affirms that illicit intercourse will not produce mixed-blooded offspring but pure Adamic stock. The following are his words: "The morals of man may be corrupted by illicit intercourse between the sexes, but the offspring will be of pure Adamic stock whether the relations of parents were legitimate or otherwise. Hence as long as man's sexual relations are confined to the Adamic family—to the flesh of men—their genealogy will be perfect and the line of descent uncorrupted."—Page 155. So according to Mr. Carroll's own teaching the word confusion in Lev. 20:12 has no reference to the corruption of offspring. Then may we not as well say that the same word in Lev. 18:23 has no reference to the corruption of offspring, but simply to the filthy mixing up of intercourse with lower animals?

I would observe also that in the LXX. the word abomination is used in Lev. 18:23 instead of confusion; also the word quadruped occurs there instead of beast. So in the LXX. the text reads: "Neither shall thou lie with any quadruped for copulation to be polluted with it, neither shall a woman present herself before any quadruped to have connection with it; for it is an abomination." This rendering brings out the idea that any unbiased thinking mind can grasp from the authorized version; namely, that God is forbidding intercourse with quadrupeds.   The use of the word quadruped in the LXX. seems to refute the idea advanced by Carroll, that the apes are bipeds.   To forbid intercourse with quadrupeds only would naturally lead us to believe that God considers the human being as the only biped animal.

But concerning offspring, it is entirely impossible that there can be any mixture of the human family with lower animals.   Paul's declaration that there are four kinds of flesh, "one kind of flesh of men, another of beasts, another of fishes, and another of birds" (1 Cor. 15:49), is an unanswerable proof of this fact. The laws of procreation can only act in cases where there is a striking similarity of flesh; but where two distinct kinds of flesh come together there can be no procreation.   Therefore, since the flesh of men is of one kind, and the flesh of beasts is of another kind, it is entirely impossible that there can be any cross between them.   We might as well think of crossing fishes with birds, or of a mixture of birds with beasts, or of beasts with fishes, as to think of producing a mixture between man and beast.   Such a thing has never occurred, and never will occur—because it never can occur.

But it is a remarkable fact that everything in the animal kingdom breeds true to its kind.   Every spe-

cies of birds or of fishes or of animals breeds true to its
kind. There can be certain crosses produced in the
animal kingdom, but it is only between animals that
are very similar in their creation, which would indicate
that they had originated from one species. This is
true in certain animals of the cat kind, also in certain
animals of the bovine kind, also in certain animals of
the dog kind, wild and domestic, also in animals of
the horse kind, etc. But there are certain species of
ainmals which are so very distinct that a cross
can not be produced between them. But many of the
crosses produced in the animal kingdom are not
fertile, in fact a vast majority of them; but there is
nothing of this kind seen in the human family.
Every mixture of what we now call the races of men
is as truly fertile as their ancestors on either side,
whether it be a cross between the white and black race,
white and yellow, white and red, white and brown, or
the black, red, brown, or yellow with any of the other
colors. This is an unanswerable proof that all these
races belong to the same species. How can our author
say the Negro is a beast and that he has the same kind
of flesh as the lower animals, when the Negro breeds
true to the human family, and not to the animals?
Many times our author unceremoniously pronounces
the Negro an ape. How can he make him out an ape,

when he will not breed with the ape kind? If the Negro were a species of ape, he would breed true to the ape kind, but would not mix with the blood of the human family. So, from every standpoint we are compelled to discard Mr. Carroll's opinion, that the Negro is a beast.

Truly there are four kinds of flesh, as the apostle Paul taught; and from the time God created this world with its inhabitants of men, beasts, birds, and fishes, there has been no amalgamation of these distinct kinds. The flesh of fishes has always been distinct from the flesh of birds, beasts, and men. The flesh of birds has always been distinct from the flesh of fishes, beasts, and men. The flesh of beasts has always been distinct from fishes, birds, and men. And the flesh of men has always been distinct from fishes, birds, and *beasts*. And believing, as I devoutly do, that the apostle's declaration concerning the four kinds of flesh is an inspired declaration and signifies a wide distinction between the flesh of men, beasts, birds, and fishes, I am not troubled with any fears of amalgamation in the future.

The reason there can be no amalgamation of the flesh of beasts, birds, and fishes, is not so well understood as the reason why there can be no amalgamation of the human family with these three kinds of flesh.

Men possess immortal souls, but none of the other three kinds of flesh possess immortal souls; and therefore the utter impossibility of amalgamation of the human family with these other kinds of flesh. This is a barrier to Mr. Carroll's theory. But from the tenor of his book I gather that he thinks he has successfully bridged over it in his explanation of the conception of a cross between the Caucasian and the Negro, which is as follows: "When sexual union takes place each side or part of these two creations, matter and mind, are united and perfected in the female, conception and birth ensues, and the combination of matter and mind is reproduced in the offspring."—Page 131.

To understand Mr. Carroll here the reader must bear in mind that he teaches the Negro to be a mere animal composed of mind and matter, without a soul, while man is composed of mind, matter, and soul. The sexual union, therefore, that he is speaking of between the Negro and the Causcasian is as follows: In the act the matter and mind in man unite with the matter and mind of the Negro and produce an offspring composed of matter and mind, but the soul in the germ of man lies dormant and does not produce a soul in the offspring. The same would be true according to his theory in case of intercourse of a male Negro with a female Caucasian. The matter and mind of which the male Negro is composed would unite with the matter and mind of a Caucasian woman and produce an offspring composed of matter and mind, without a soul — the soul in the germ of woman remaining dormant.

Again we see Mr. Carroll running himself into difficulties. If the Negro is composed of mind and matter only and has no soul, and all the lower animals possess the same mind that man possesses, there is no reason why the Negro will not amalgamate with some of the lower species of animals. And if the matter and mind in the germ of man can be used independent of the immortal element to produce the offspring by amalgamation with one creature who consists only of mortal elements, there is no reason why he will not amalgamate with other species of the lower animals in the same way. Our author can not disprove these facts. It is perfectly unreasonable to suppose that a creature could amalgamate with another creature which does not possess like elements in its germ. One had as well talk about producing a chemical combination without the proper elements in due proportion. I say it is ridiculously absurd to talk about a creature possessing both mortal and immortal elements uniting by amalgamation with a creature that possesses only mortal elements. Such a thing never has occured, and never will. .

A cross between man and any of the lower animals would refute the doctrine that man has an immortal entity; but there is no danger of such a cross, since the flesh of men is one kind, and the flesh of animals is another kind. Since it is impossible for an amalgamation of man who possess immortal mind and immortal soul, with any creature who does not possess these immortal elements, it is evident that every creature with which he will amalgamate possesses them. If the Negro, therefore, is not a man, he must be a beast which possesses the immortal elements, because he breeds true to man. But since there are no beasts that possess immortal minds, or immortal souls, the Negro can not be a beast, because he possesses both. Only men possess immortal minds, or immortal souls; therefore, the Negro is a man. As beasts can not amalgamate with the human family, the Negro is not a beast, because he can and does amalgamate.

I will now take up Mr. Carroll's twists upon a number of texts of scripture which he uses to prove that God's judgment has been poured out upon the human family in various instances because of their amalgamation with the Negro, or beast, as he styles him. He holds that amalgamation with the Negro was the principal sin that brought the deluge upon the world.

Concerning this he says: "Prior to the deluge God looked upon the earth and said it was corrupt; for all flesh had corrupted his way upon the earth. God thus describes the condition of the flesh of the earth, which could only have resulted from amalgamation."—Page 159.

Our author means to teach here that the corruption of all flesh prior to the flood signified that the blood of the entire human family, or nearly so, had become mixed with a species of beast, which he says was the Negro. The words here quoted from his book imply that the flesh can not become corrupted in any other way; but in this he makes a great mistake. Corrupt flesh throughout the Bible signifies sinful flesh. There is no corruption of human flesh mentioned in the Bible that signifies anything else than sinful flesh. If the expression "corrupt flesh" in the Bible always signifies a flesh composed of a mixture of man and beast, there would be no possibility of a man defiling or corrupting his own flesh by any sin he might commit against God. Now we know that every sin that man commits against God brings upon him a moral corruption; therefore, to maintain his theory, our author is driven to take the stand that the soul of a man only is corrupted by sin, and not his body. Such a stand would be as ridiculous as the rest of his ideas.

It is impossible that a man may sink his soul into a morally corrupted state and his body remain uncorrupted. When a man lifts his hand to sin against God, condemnation rests upon his entire being, mind, soul, and body. When the nature of man became corrupted in the fall, he became morally corrupted in soul, body, and mind. This is proven by the fact that when man is pointed to Christ for redemption from his sinful condition it is shown that he is to receive a cleansing of soul, body, and mind; as, for instance, in 2 Cor. 7:1 the apostle Paul says, "Having therefore these promises, dearly beloved, let us cleanse ourselves from all filthiness of the flesh and spirit, perfecting holiness in the fear of God." We see by this that the flesh as well as the spirit of man is defiled by sin. Therefore, when God looked upon the antediluvians and saw that all flesh had corrupted his (God's) way, he found them in a state of moral pollution of mind, soul, and body, by sinful practices; and because they were waxing worse and worse in their sins the God of justice thought best to destroy them. Noah at that time found favor in the eyes of God because he was righteous and perfect in his uprightness and in his ways before God, and sinned not against God as did other antediluvians. There is not a shadow of proof that the deluge was sent upon the antediluvians because of their amalgamation with some species of beast, or that any such amalgamation in any way helped to call down the wrath of God upon them.

Our author holds also that amalgamation with the Negro was the chief sin that brought God's judgment upon the cities of Sodom and Gomorrah and the country round about. He likewise holds that it was the chief sin that brought God's judgment at different times upon the Israelites. As there is no door through which he can enter the Bible with his erroneous idea, he tries hard to make one by a certain notable twist upon the words adultery and fornication. He endeavors to show that adultery includes all the sins that the human family may commit by unlawful intercourse with each other, and that fornication is an offense which men and women commit when they associate themselves carnally with the Negro. The following quotation from his book will give the reader a clear understanding of his teaching regarding this matter.

"It will be observed that the Bible describes two offences which result from illicit intercourse between the sexes; the one is termed adultery, and the other fornication. The modern world has been taught to believe that adultery is unfaithfulness of any married

person to the marriage bed (Webster's Dictionary) and
that fornication is the intercourse or lewdness of un-
married persons, male or female (Ibid). This is opposed to the teachings of scripture. Our Savior said:
'It hath been said, Whosoever shall put away his wife,
saving for the cause of fornication, causeth her to commit adultery; and whosoever shall marry her . . . com-
mitteth adultery.'—Matt. 5:32. Here we observe the
distinction made between fornication and adultery and
that a person may commit fornication; and if for any
other cause save fornication a man put away his wife
and another man marries her, both the woman and the
man whom she marries commit adultery, but not
fornication. As has been shown, Cain and other
antediluvians and the people of Sodom and Gomorrah
and the Israelites were all charged by Jude with committing fornication and going. after strange flesh.
Adultery is that offence which men and women commit
by illicit intercourse with their own kind of flesh; and
fornication is that offence which men and women
commit when they associate themselves carnally with
the Negro or with the mixed-bloods; that is, with
strange flesh. The New Testament abounds with
denunciations of fornication and fornicators, which
indicates that fornication was prevalent in the days of
the Savior and that, like the prophets who preceded

him, his mission was to break up this wicked,
destructive practice and the social, political, and
religious equality with the Negro which inevitably
leads to it, and to restore the relation of master and
servant which God established between man and the
Negro in the creation."—Pages 311, 312.

The reader will observe how our author admits in
this place that his definition of the words adultery
and fornication is not in harmony with Webster's
Dictionary. Now I am very certain that our diction-
aries define these words according to the true signification in our language. If therefore that which is
translated fornication in our Bible signifies illicit
intercourse with some creature outside the human
family, it should be translated by an English word
which has such a signification, and not by the word
fornication; for no such signification is attached to
that word in our language. But our author does not
criticize the translation. He never hints that the
Authorized Version is translated erroneously in the
places where the word fornication occurs. He simply
tries to suddenly spring upon the people a new definition for these words. I am sure I am ready to accept
all the light it is possible to obtain upon the holy
scriptures; but I can not accept as a definition of an
English term that has been in use for hundreds of

years, an idea that has never been attached to it by any author.

In the New Testament the word fornication is always translated from *porneia*, and the word adultery from *moicheia*. It is difficult to maintain the distinction between these two words that is perfectly carried out in the King James' version. It seems that both these words in the original may signify every phase of whoredom. But, however this may be, it is very evident that both these words are sometimes applied to the same sinful act in Greek literature. We have an example of this in Rev. 2:21, 22. "And I gave her space to repent of her fornication [*porneia*], and she repented not. Behold, I will cast her into a bed, and they that commit adultery [*moicheia*] with her into great tribulation except they repent of their deeds." If the sinful act mentioned here was criminal intercourse with beasts, it is evident that such intercourse is styled adultery as well as fornication, and our author's theory is overthrown. And if the sin referred to here was criminal intercourse between human beings on both sides, it is evident that such intercourse between two human beings is called fornication, as well as adultery, and our author's theory is overthrown. So we have him in another dilemma. If he takes the *stand* that Jezebel was a Negress, he opposes his theory, because the text calls her a woman, and he holds that Negresses are female beasts, and not women. And if he takes the stand that those who committed this sinful act with Jezebel were Negroes, he again refutes his theory, because he holds that Negroes are beasts, and do not possess souls; but these persons had been Christians and dwelt in the church at Thyatira, hence must have possessed immortal souls.

That fornication can have no reference in its scriptural use to criminal intercourse of men with beasts, is evident from the Authorized Version alone. In 1 Cor. 5:1 we read: "It is reported commonly that there is fornication among you, and such fornication as is not so much as named among the Gentiles, that one should have his father's wife." Here is fornication without a Negro connected with it, but it was a Corinthian who actually made use of his father's wife. The one who committed this offense was not a beast, either, because in the fifth verse Paul instructs the Corinthians to deliver the offender unto Satan for the destruction of the flesh, that the spirit may be saved in the day of the Lord Jesus. So he had an immortal spirit—hence was a man.

Also in 1 Cor. 10:8 we read: "Neither let us commit fornication, as some of them also committed, and fell in *one day* three and twenty thousand." The fornication mentioned here is that which the young men of Israel committed with the young women that king Balak, by the instructions of the prophet Balaam, sent out to tempt the Israelites. Were these ladies Negresses? No; because this whoredom was committed with the daughters of Moab. See Num. 25:1. The Moabites were not Negroes nor mixed-bloods, but true descendants of Moab, who was the son of Lot by his eldest daughter, and Lot was Abraham's brother's son. That the Moabites had not amalgamated with any species of beasts down to the time of Moses, is evident from Gen. 19:36, 37, which says: "Thus were both the daughters of Lot with child by their father. And the first bare a son, and called his name Moab; the same is the father of the Moabites unto this day." So there had been no amalgamation among the Moabites down to the time that the children of Israel committed whoredom with them. Therefore our author can not evade the fact that fornication is a sin committed by two human beings.

If he wants to make us believe that God overthrew Sodom and Gomorrah and the cities of Israel because of their amalgamation with a species of beast, he must find some better proof than the mere fact that they committed fornication. It might be well to consider *in this place* the record of Sodom's sins handed down

to us by the prophet Ezekiel, who, when rebuking
Jerusalem for her iniquities, denominated her the
sister of Sodom. The following are his words: "And
thine elder sister is Samaria, she and her daughters
that dwell at thy left hand: and thy younger sister,
that dwelleth at thy right hand, is Sodom and her
daughters." — Eze. 16:46. "Behold, this was the
iniquity of thy sister Sodom, pride, fulness of bread,
and abundance of idleness was in her and in her
daughters, neither did she strengthen the hand of the
poor and needy. And they were haughty, and committed abomination before me: therefore I took them
away as I saw good."—Verses 49, 50. No amalgamation with beasts is mentioned in this record of the sins
of Sodom. The Sodomites were destroyed because of
their pride, gluttony, idleness, neglect of the poor,
haughtiness, and the abomination which they committed.

If I were going to produce a catalogue of the sins of
Sodom that are included in the word abomination, in
the record of Sodom's sins handed down to us by the
prophet, I would endeavor to make the people of this
day understand the prophet as the people of his own
day understood him. To do this I must turn to the
law of Moses and show how many things were pronounced an abomination to the Israelites. In the

18th chapter of Leviticus these abominations are upon record. This chapter first forbids the marriage of a near relative. Verses 6-18. Then it forbids the approach of a man unto a menstruous woman. Ver. 19. Next it forbids whoredom. Ver. 20. Next it forbids Israel to allow their seed to pass through the fire to Moloch. Ver. 21. Next it forbids sodomy in the following words: "Thou shalt not lie with mankind as with womankind."—Ver. 22. Next it forbids illicit intercourse with beasts. Ver. 23. Next it is stated that for these sins already mentioned the Canaanites were driven out of their land before Israel, in the following words: "Defile not ye yourselves in any of these things; for in all these the nations are defiled which I cast out before you: and the land is defiled: therefore I do visit the iniquity thereof upon it, and the land itself vomiteth out her inhabitants." So the iniquity of the Canaanites was not, as our author would have it, the procreation of creatures half man and half beast, but the committing of the abominations mentioned above, which does not so much as hint at the procreation of a seed by amalgamation with animals.

Next God says to the Israelites: "Ye shall therefore keep my statutes and my judgments, and shall not commit any of these abominations; neither any of your own nation, nor any stranger that sojourneth among you (for all these abominations have the men of the land done, which were before you, and the land is defiled); that the land spue not you out also, when ye defile it, as it spued out the nations that were before you. For whosoever shall commit any of these abominations, even the souls that commit them shall be cut off from among their people. Therefore shall ye keep mine ordinance, that ye commit not any one of these abominable customs, which are committed before you, and that ye defile not yourselves therein: I am the Lord your God."—Lev. 18:26-30.

This scripture fully sets forth the idea of an abomination unto Israel, and, as we before stated, there is no hint at the production of offspring by amalgamation with beasts. So when Ezekiel wrote to the Israelites that the Sodomites had committed abomination, they understood him to say that they had committed one or more of these wicked things described in this chapter. They understood that they had either made marriages with near relatives, or had approached menstruous women, or had committed adultery, or caused their seed to pass through the fire to Moloch, or men had lain with men, or they had lain with beasts; or that they had done all these things. We have no proof that the people of Sodom did all these abominations, neither have we proof that they did not commit all these abominations. But we have proof that they committed at least three of these abomination; namely, sodomy, fornication (whoredom in all its phases), and going after strange flesh, which doubtless refers to the lying of men with beasts. That they committed sodomy is evident from the fact that the men of Sodom were bent on performing this lewd act with the angels who lodged in the house of Lot the night before the destruction of the city. See Gen. 19. Paul describes this abominable practice as follows: "And likewise also the men, leaving the natural use of the woman, burned in their lust one toward another; men with men working that which is unseemly, and receiving in themselves that recompense of their error which was meet."—Rom. 1:27. This unlawful act of men with men was so abundant among the Sodomites that it bears their name until this day.

I will now consider the arguments brought forth by our author to prove that amalgamation with the Negro was the chief sin that brought the judgments of God upon Israel at various times. To establish this idea he argues as follows: "The following charge of the Almighty is one of the many with which the Scriptures abound, which go to prove that the Israelites violated the law of God and descended to amalgamation with the Negroes and with the mixed-bloods. 'For mine eyes are upon all their ways. . . . And first I will recompense their iniquity and their sin double; because they have defiled my land, they have filled mine inheritance with the carcasses of their detestable and abominable things.'—Jer. 16:17, 18.   Thus the Isrealites, like the antediluvians and the Canaanites, defiled the land.   What is God's inheritance? Israel was God's inheritance (See 1 Kings 8:51; Isa. 19:25, etc.).   Then by their amalgamation they had defiled the land, and had filled .Israel—the nation of Israel—with the carcasses of things that were detestable and abominable in the sight of God.   Observe that in producing those detestable and abominable things they had defiled the land just as the Canaanites had done. Observe also that the Creator of the heaven and the earth, the maker of man and beast, he who fashioned the fowl of the air, and the fish of the sea—God—the Author of all language and all speech—declined to give the name of this loathsome offspring of man and the Negro, and the nearest that he would come to naming them is found in his declination recorded in our text, when, in the absence of all name (for these monstrosities are nameless) he bestows upon them the descriptive epithet 'detestable and abominable things.'

"The above text throws a flood of light upon God's

command to Jeremiah. 'Thou shalt not take thee a wife, neither shalt thou have sons or daughters in this place. For thus saith the Lord concerning the sons and concerning the daughters that are born in this place, and concerning their mothers that bare them, and concerning their father's that begat them in this land; they shall die of grievous deaths; they shall not be lamented; neither shall they be buried; but they shall be as dung upon the face of the earth: and they shall be consumed by the sword, and by famine; and their carcasses shall be meat for the fowls of heaven, and for the beasts of the earth.'—Jer. 16:2-4. We are thus taught (1) that the men of Israel had persisted in amalgamation so long that their male progeny of mixed-bloods were not discernable from pure whites, and that in this way many of the women of Israel had been led into amalgamation; hence it was dangerous for a man to take a wife from among them, and Jeremiah was forbidden to do so. (2) That in the eyes of God the offspring of man and the Negro was only fit for dung on the face of the earth.''—Pages 209-210.

We have here another example of our author's inability to comprehend the scriptures. There is not a hint at amalgamation with the Negroes or mixed-bloods either in the texts he quoted or their context.

It was not because Israel had descended to amalgamation with Negroes that Jeremiah was forbidden to take a wife from among them. But the reason is plainly stated in the text he quotes; namely, "Thus saith the Lord concerning the sons and concerning the daughters that are born in this place; they shall die grievous deaths," etc. It was because an awful judgment was to come from God upon the Jews so soon that the prophet was instructed not to take a wife and endeavor to bring up children among them. Sure enough, it was but a short time until this prophecy came true; for at the hands of the Babylonians the Jews were slaughtered with a great slaughter, and the surviving ones were carried off into captivity. Had Jeremiah ignored this instruction of the Almighty and taken a wife and endeavored to bring up sons and daughters, he would doubtless have been brought to sorrow by having his wife and daughters slaughtered as many other mothers and daughters were slaughtered in Judah. This is the only reason assigned why God instructed Jeremiah not to take a wife from among the Jews.

But what was the sin for which this judgment was to have been meted out to Israel? It is evident that it was not for one kind of sin, because the very text quoted by our author speaks of their wickedness in the plural, as follows: "Mine eyes are upon all their ways." This shows that there were various sins that Israel had been committing, for which God was going to send punishment upon them. This text as it stands in the LXX. mentions the transgression of Judah in the plural in several places. I will quote it. "For mine eyes are upon all their ways, and their iniquities have not been hidden from mine eyes, and I will recompense their mischiefs double and their sins whereby they have profaned my land with the carcasses of their abominations, and with their iniquities whereby they have trespassed against mine inheritance." To say that one sin of Israel is denounced here more than any other sin is simply to betray a biased mind. God was reproving them for all their sins, which beyond doubt were many. The carcasses of detestable and abominable things mentioned in the Authorized Version is translated "the carcasses of their abominations" in the LXX. The Jews had filled God's inheritance with these carcasses, according to the Authorized Version, and they had defiled God's land with them, according to the LXX. But it makes but little difference which of the versions we follow; for they both contain the same idea. The land of Israel had been sanctified by Jehovah for the holy *people* to dwell in, hence it was a holy land; and any

sin committed in that land is considered, in the light
of the Old Testament, a defilement of the land. Israel
was a sanctified people unto Jehovah, hence a holy
land was required for them to dwell in. Any sin,
therefore, that they might commit, defiled not only
themselves as a people, but the land also in which they
dwelt. It was impossible for them to have defiled their
land without defiling themselves; and it was impossible
for them to defile themselves without defiling the
land. Whether, therefore, we conclude that the sins
of Israel had defiled Israel or had defiled the land in
which they dwelt, we have the same idea morally.
The carcasses, however, were but one kind of the evil
things that abounded in Judah.

But what were they? This the context explains to us perfectly. I marvel that our author was
unable to grasp this explanation. In verse twenty,
which is but the second verse below where he left off
quoting, the prophet says, "Shall a man make gods
unto himself, and they are no gods?" This explains
these carcasses perfectly. They were idols that Israel
had made of wood and stone in disobedience to the
first commandment, which said, "Thou shalt have no
other gods before me"; also in disobedience to the
second commandment, which forbade them to make
any image or likeness of anything in heaven or in the
earth to worship the same.

This same defilement of the land by the worship of the images is spoken of elsewhere in the Bible. In Jer. 3:9 we read: "And it came to pass through the lightness of her whoredom, that she defiled the land, and committed adultery with stones and with stocks." This committing adultery with stones and stocks signified the worshiping of images made of wood and stone.

Also, in Eze. 43:7 we read: "And he said unto me, Son of man, the place of my throne, and the place of the soles of my feet, where I will dwell in the midst of the children of Israel forever, and my holy name shall the house of Israel no more defile, neither they, nor their kings, by their whoredom, nor by the carcasses of their kings in their high places." The carcasses mentioned here are called carcasses of their kings. Doubtless they deified some of the kings after their death, as was common among the heathen round about, and made images unto them and worshiped them. In verse nine of the same chapter, God says, "Now let them put away their whoredom, and the carcasses of their kings, far from me, and I will dwell in the midst of them forever." You see, there is no mention of any mixed-bloods among the Israelites in any of the metaphoric expressions referred to by our author. This idea is begotten in the imagination of *his own* heart.

We now come to mixed marriages among the Jews.
Our author would have us believe that the reason God
forbade the Jews to make marriages with the various
nations of Canaan, was that they were mixed-bloods,
and not pure Adamic stock.   But in this he is again
mistaken, because the Scriptures explain very clearly
the reason this command was given, and there is no
reference to mixed-bloods connected with it.   I will
quote the verses that contain the command and the
reason why it was given.   "When the Lord thy God
shall bring thee into the land whither thou goest to
possess it, and hath cast out many nations before thee,
the Hittites, and the Girgashites, and the Amorites,
and the Canaanites, and the Perizzites, and the
Hivites, and the Jebusites, seven nations greater and
mightier than thou: and when the Lord thy God shall
deliver them before thee; thou shalt smite them, and
utterly destroy them; thou shalt make no covenant
with them, nor show mercy unto them: neither shalt
thou make marriages with them; thy daughter thou
shalt not give unto his son, nor his daughter shalt
thou take unto thy son.   For they will turn away thy
son from following me, that they may serve other
gods: so will the anger of the Lord be kindled against
you, and destroy thee suddenly.   But thus shall ye
deal with them; ye shall destroy their altars, and

break down their images, and cut down their groves, and burn their graven images with fire."—Deut. 7:1-5.

The reason marriages were forbidden the Jews with the heathen nations is plainly set forth here; namely, "they will turn away thy sons from following me, that they may serve other gods." If this command had been given because these heathen nations were not pure Adamic stock, God would have told us so; but he did not say he gave the command for any such reason. The only reason assigned was the danger of their mixed marriages leading them away from God to serve other gods; that is, idols, such as these nations worshiped.

The Jews did not always obey this command, and sometimes made marriages with the heathen nations. The result was just what God told them it would be; namely, they were led into idolatry. This was true in the case of king Solomon, who allowed his heart to run out after heathen women until he was induced to make marriages with them; and we are told that they turned away his heart from the true God after the gods of the heathen. See 1 Kings 11. This is the only reason assigned anywhere in the writings of the Old Testament why God forbade the Jews to make marriages with the heathen nations. But when these *heathen* nations came and united with the Jewish church, by renouncing all the heathen gods and swearing allegiance to the true God, and received the rite of circumcision and became true Jewish proselytes, they were allowed to make marriages with them because they then became their true Jewish brethren. But our author would have us believe that the doors of the Jewish church were closed against certain heathen nations because they were not of pure Adamic stock; but he says on page 243 of his book, "Its doors stood open to all the pure Adamic stock. Every pure-booded descendant of Adam could become a member of the Jewish church and participate in its benefit by complying with the law on the subject."

Let us investigate these words of our author and see if they teach the truth.   If the doors of the Jewish church were closed against the nations who were made up of creatures that were mixed-boods, half man and half beast, and were open to all the pure-blooded stock of Adam, let us try and find out by the Bible how many of the ancient nations were composed of mixed-bloods, and how many of pure Adamic stock.   The injunction which closed the door of the Jewish church against certain heathen nations is found in Deut. 23: 3-8, which I quote: "An Ammonite or Moabite shall not enter into the congregation [church] of the Lord; even to their tenth generation shall they not enter into

the congregation of the Lord forever: because they
met you not with bread and with water in the way,
when ye came forth out of Egypt; and because they
hired against thee Balaam the son of Beor, of Pethor
of Mesopotamia, to curse thee.   Nevertheless the
Lord thy God would not harken unto Balaam; but
the Lord thy God turned the curse into a blessing unto
thee, because the Lord thy God loved thee.   Thou
shalt not seek their peace nor their prosperity all thy
days forever.   Thou shalt not abhor an Edomite; for
he is thy brother: thou shalt not abhor an Egyptian,
because thou wast a stranger in his land.   The
children that are begotten of them shall enter into
the congregation of the Lord in their third generation.''

There is no other injunction in Moses' law that
closed the doors of the Jewish church against any
nation of people; therefore, the only barrier to
entrance into the Jewish church is found in this text
and what is contained in it; namely, the Ammonites
and the Moabites were not allowed to enter the Jewish
church.   No other nations were rejected.   Observe
that even the Egyptians were allowed to enter the
Jewish church in their third generation.   The reader
will bear in mind that our author holds the Egyptians
as a nation of mixed-bloods.   If they were mixed-

bloods, then mixed-bloods were allowed to come and join the Jewish church. Not only the Egyptians, but also the seven nations of the land of Canaan, the Hittites, the Amorites, the Girgashites, the Canaanites, the Perizzites, the Hivites, and the Jebusites, were all allowed to become members of the Jewish church. Also the Ethiopians and all the black races of Africa, and all other nations except the Ammonites and the Moabites, were allowed to come and join the Jewish church by complying with the law of circumcision and renouncing their false gods and accepting the true God of Israel. But why were the Moabites and the Ammonites denied admission into the Jewish church? Is it because they were mixed-bloods? No; they were not mixed-bloods. The Ammonites were the descendants of Benamni, who was Lot's son by his youngest daughter; and the Moabites were the descendants of Moab, who was Lot's son by his eldest daughter. So they were pure Adamic stock and could not have been rejected because they were mixed-bloods. But the text before us tells us why they were rejected. The reason is as follows: "Because they met you not with bread and with water in the way, when ye came forth out of Egypt; and because they hired against thee Balaam the son of Beor of Pethor of Mesopotamia, to curse thee."—Deut. 23:4. This is very plain. We need not misunderstand it. No mention is made of mixed-bloods. This all comes from the imagination of our author's own heart.

We have many examples of the Gentiles gaining admission into the Jewish church, in the Old Testament writings. We read of a great revival that the Jews had while they were in Babylon, which resulted in gaining many converts from the Babylonians. The record is as follows: "The Jews had light, and gladness, and joy, and honor. And in every province, and in every city, whithersoever the king's commandment and his decree came, the Jews had joy and gladness, a feast and a good day. And many of the people of the land became Jews; for the fear of the Jews fell upon them."—Esther 8:16, 17.

In the time of David also, in the Jewish church were converts from the heathen nations. One of his soldiers, namely, Uriah, was a Hittite. The Hittites were one of the seven nations that God cast out of Canaan by the hands of the Isrealites. This proves that even the nations that inhabited Canaan could and did become members of the Jewish church. God never hinted to Israel that it was wrong. He sent no curses upon David for having Uriah among his people; but when David took measures to kill him (which *would* have been right according to our author's theory, because he says these Hittites were mixed-bloods, and that mixed-bloods have no right to live), God punished him severely.

But something worse than we have yet mentioned is connected with the story of Uriah, according to our author's theory. Uriah the Hittite was married to a Jewess by the name of Bathsheba. We are told in 2 Sam. 11:3 that she was the daughter of Eliam; the margin has it Ammiel. Ammiel was of the tribe of Dan. Num. 13:12. So this is a clear case of a Jewess marrying a man of Gentile blood, even a cursed Hittite; yet there is nothing in the Bible that would lead us to believe that God was displeased with this marriage. If our author's theory were true, Bathsheba would have committed a most shocking crime by marrying Uriah the Hittite, because he tells us that the Hittites, with the six other nations that inhabited Canaan, were all destroyed by God because they had descended to amalgamation with the Negroes until they were no longer the pure stock of Adam. If, therefore, his theory be true, Bathsheba married a mixed-blood; and our author tells us she committed the crime that Moses forbade in the eighteenth chapter of Leviticus, when he said unto the Jews, "Thou shalt not lie with any beast to defile thyself therewith; neither shall any woman stand before any beast to lie down thereto."—Ver. 23. Whosoever committed this sin was to be put to death, whether male or female. Lev. 20:15, 16. Therefore, according to our author's theory, Bathsheba should have been put to death; also, it was perfectly right for David to kil[l] Uriah, since, according to our author's theory, he was part beast; for we read that in case a woman lies with a beast, both the woman and the beast should be killed. Lev. 20:16. But it is very evident that our author's theory is not true, because God, rather than approving of David's action in the murder of Uriah, sent a severe judgment upon him.

But there is something still worse connected with this story, if our author's theory be true. King David lusted after this woman, who, according to our author's theory, had lain with a beast; and after he had caused the murder of Uriah he married her, and of this woman begot Solomon. When we read that Solomon is one of the ancestors of the Messiah, we are driven to say that there is a great stain upon the lineage of Christ, if our author's theory be true.

There is another case of mixed marriage in the Bible that stains the holy seed according to our author's theory. We have seen that the Moabites and the Ammonites were the only nations that were forever barred from the Jewish church. The Egyptians were barred for two generations, but in the third generation they were allowed to enter the Jewish church. So if there was any mixed-blood in the Egyptians, God supposed it would be all bred out before the third generation. But our author's theory is that it would never breed out. Were these two nations, as our author's theory teaches, barred from a membership in the Jewish church because they were mixed-bloods, and not of the pure Adamic stock? We answer again, No; they were of pure Adamic stock. We read in the book of Ruth of an Israelite who, with his wife and two sons, in the time of a famine, moved out of the land of Israel to the land of the Moabites. We are also told that the two sons of this Hebrew married wives from among the Moabites, one of the very nations that was barred out of the Jewish church forever. They lived in the land of the Moabites about ten years, we are told, when the man and his two sons died, leaving his wife, Naomi, and her two daughters-in-law, Orpah and Ruth (the two Moabite women that Naomi's sons had married). Naomi instructed her daughters-in-law to go back unto their people. Orpah obeyed her and went back, but Ruth clung to her, saying, "Intreat me not to leave thee, or to return from following after thee: for whither thou goest, I will go; and where thou lodgest, I will lodge: thy people shall be my people, and thy God my God: where thou diest, will I die, and there will I be buried: the Lord do so to me, and more also, if aught but death part me and thee."—1:16, 17. So Ruth clung to Naomi and went back with her to Bethlehem in the land of Israel. Afterwards she became the wife of Boaz, and by her Boaz begat Obed, who was the grandfather of king David. Now if the Moabites were mixed-bloods, Obed was a mixed-blood; and if Obed was a mixed-blood, Jesse his son was a mixed-blood; and if Jesse was a mixed-blood, David his son was a mixed-blood; and if the mixed-blood can never be bred out, as our author states, the Messiah was a mixed-blood, because he was of the seed of David. Surely the reader can see that our author's theory will not hold good in the Bible. If I were holding to a false theory like he is, it seems to me when the word of God peels it from stem to stern I would drop it.

I will yet observe, before I leave the subject of mixed marriages, that our author makes use of Abraham's opposition to his son taking a wife from among the Canaanites; how he made his servant swear that he would not take a wife unto Isaac from among the Canaanites, but that he would go to Abraham's kindred and take a wife for Isaac; also that Rebecca *and Isaac* were opposed to the idea of Jacob taking a

wife from among the Canaanites, and therefore sent
him to Padanaram to marry his cousin. Our author
says: "The explanation of all this is found in God's
charge against the Canaanites, that they lay with
beasts and thus defile their nations and defile the land;
hence their descendants were amalgamated, they were
mixed-bloods—a mingled people."—Page 302.

Here again our author has a wrong idea of the
scriptures. It was not because the Canaanites were
part beast that Abraham refused to let his son take a
wife from among them, and that Isaac and Rebecca
refused to have their son Jacob marry one of them;
but because the Canaanites were idolaters and engulfed
in wickedness, and the wives might turn away the
hearts of the sons from the true and living God. The
reader should bear in mind that Jacob's brother Esau
did marry wives from among the Canaanites. He had
at least three wives, according to the scriptural
account. One was a woman of the Hittites, and
another was a woman of the Hivites. These were two of
the nations that God cast out of the land of Canaan
before the Israelites. The third was the daughter of
Ishmael. See. Gen. 36:1-3. According to our author's
theory, two of these wives of Esau were mixed-bloods;
that is, they were part man and part beast; therefore,
the children of Esau were mixed-bloods, and, according

to our author's doctrine, had no right to live. Why then did not God visit the children of Esau with the same extermination that he visited the Hittites and the Hivites? They were evidently mixed with the blood of the Hivites and Hittites. If the Hittites and Hivites were mixed-bloods, the children of Esau were mixed-bloods also; and if the Hittites and Hivites were exterminated because they were mixed-bloods, as our author would have it, the children of Esau should have been exterminated also, because they were mixed-bloods. But they were not condemned by God, as were the Hittites and Hivites; therefore, we must look for the cause of the extermination of the Hivites and Hittites in something else than mixed blood. God was far from exterminating the children of Esau by the hand of Israel when they came out of Egypt, as is shown in the second chapter of Deuteronomy, from which I quote.

"And command thou the people, saying, Ye are to pass through the coast of your brethren the children of Esau, which dwell in Seir; and they shall be afraid of you: take ye good heed unto yourselves therefore: meddle not with them; for I will not give you of their land, no, not so much as a foot breadth; because I have given mount Seir unto Esau for a possession. *Ye shall* buy meat of them for money, that ye may eat; and ye shall also buy water of them for money, that ye may drink. . . . And when we passed by from our brethren the children of Esau, which dwelt in Seir, through the way of the plain from Elath, and from Ezion-gaber, we turned and passed by the way of the wilderness of Moab."—Verses 4-8.

Observe how the children of Esau are here twice called the brethren of the Israelites, although their blood was mixed with the blood of the accursed Canaanites. This is a proof that mixed blood had nothing to do with the destruction of the Canaanites, nor with any of the other abhorrences of the nations on record in the Bible. If our author possessed the same spirit that the Israelites possessed when they passed by mount Seir, he would be willing to call good people out of every nation, regardless of their color, his brethren, as did they. Observe with what respect the Israelites were compelled to treat the children of Esau. They were not allowed to eat any of Esau's bread without paying for it, nor even to take a drink from any of their wells without paying for the same. If these children of Esau were mixed-bloods, God surely had great respect for mixed-bloods. How different God is from Mr. Carroll, who tells us that the mixed-bloods have no rights that we dare to respect, not even the right to live!

It will be noticed that we meet with the children of Esau under another name in the Bible, viz., that of the Edomites. "And Jacob sod pottage: and Esau came from the field, and he was faint: and Esau said to Jacob, Feed me, I pray thee, with that same red pottage; for 1 am faint: therefore was his name called Edom [red]."—Gen. 25:29, 30. "Now these are the generations of Esau, who is Edom."— Gen. 36:1. "Thus dwelt Esau in mount Seir: Esau is Edom."—Ver. 8. "And these are the generations of Esau the father of the Edomites in mount Seir." —Ver. 9. These texts prove that the Edomites of whom we read in the Bible were the same people as the children of Esau.

Now let us observe how Moses opens the door of the Jewish church to the Edomites. "Thou shalt not abhor an Edomite; for he is thy brother: thou shalt not abhor an Egyptian; because thou wast a stranger in his land. The children that are begotten of them shall enter into the congregation [church] of the Lord in their third generation."—Deut. 23:7, 8. According to Mr. Carroll's theory, Moses opened the doors of the Jewish church to a despicable race of mixed-blooded apes. Without commenting any further, the reader can see that there is no truth in Mr. Carroll's *theory*, that Abraham and Isaac refused to save their

sons marry the Canaanites because they were mixed-
bloods. Their real object, as we stated before, was
the fear that the women of Canaan should lead their
sons away from the true God.

PERVERSIONS OF THE GOSPEL.

Mr. Carroll's theory not only twists the sacred records of the Old Testament from beginning to end, but also introduces the most shameful and obnoxious perversions of the gospel of our Savior. The gospel of Christ was to be preached to all nations (Matt. 28:19), and unto every creature. Mark 16:15. This proves that the doors of Christ's church were opened unto every class of humanity. Peter found this to be true, hence he exclaimed in Acts 10:34, 35 —"Of a truth I perceive that God is no respecter of persons; but in every nation he that feareth him, and worketh righteousness, is accepted with him."

Christ came into this world to make an atonement that was capable of saving the entire human family, and we read concerning this atonement in Heb. 2:9, that he by the grace of God tasted death for every man. This sublime declaration of the apostle shows that God looks upon all nations, races, and colors of the human family alike, and that Jesus Christ has shed his blood as much for the black, red, brown, or *yellow* man as for the white man. These are barriers to Mr. Carroll's doctrine, so he tries to evade these plain and glorious truths by the claim that the blacks, reds, browns, and yellows are not men, but beasts and mixed-blooded apes.   Hear what he says about them.

"The mere fact that under the influence of the law of hereditary the ultimate offspring of whites and negroes when mated continuously with white persons to a greater or less extent the elevated physical and mental characters of the white does not make them men and women.   They lack the spiritual creation which forms the link of kinship between God and man and is only transmittable to his offspring through pure Adamic channels.   Nothing could be more absurd, nothing more blasphemous, than to suppose that God who declines to establish any kinship between himself and the animals would make it possible for man to do so by an act which of itself is a violation of that divine law 'thou shalt not lie with any beast'; hence the mixed-bloods and corrupted flesh inherit none of the immortality of their Adamic parent—they have no soul—but, like the Negro and the rest of the animals, they are merely combinations of matter and mind. They were not in existence at the time of Adam's transgression and are not included in the plan of salvation.   Man alone fell, and he alone is the subject of redemption."—Pages 155, 156.

Did ever such vile and blasphemous words drop from the lips of man! This is a doctrine of devils unmasked. Oh, shame on the man who without a straw of evidence to prove his base and wicked theory would assert that only the Caucasian race is included in the atonement! God be merciful to such a sinner. Such an idea alone, if entertained, would prevent a human soul from descending into that true contrition and humility necessary to obtain salvation. Such downright prejudice and hatred against the colored races would bar any human soul out of heaven and send it to eternal damnation where dwell both white and colored races who have rejected the gospel and atonement of our Savior. But Mr. Carroll actually tries to twist the scriptures of the New Testament into a proof that the commission of Christ—"Go ye into all the world, and preach the gospel to every creature"—was limited to the Caucasian race. He fixes up the commission as follows:

" 'Go ye into all the world, and preach the gospel to every creature' (Mark 16:15), remembering that God 'hath made of one blood all nations of men' (Acts 17:26); but 'give not that which is holy unto the dogs, neither cast ye your pearls before swine, lest they trample them under their feet, and turn again and rend you.'—Matt. 7:5. The existence of this prohibitory statute demonstrates the existence of an animal which man in his criminal ignorance of God's plan of creation might mistake for a man, and thus be misled into giving him the Bible with a view of conferring upon him the blessings of Christianity, which were intended alone for man. When we view this statute in the light of the sciences and in that of Paul's declaration that there is one kind of flesh of men, another flesh of beasts, etc., it becomes plain that the dog and the swine and the Negro all belong to the same kind of flesh—the flesh of beasts. The Scriptures are described as holy (Rom. 1:2, etc.), the kingdom of heaven is compared to goodly pearls (Matt. 13:45, 46): hence we are led to decide that that which is holy and that which man is forbidden to give unto dogs, is the Bible, and that the pearls which man is forbidden to cast unto swine is the kingdom of heaven. This statute was evidently designed to confine the use of the Bible and religious worship to men, and exclude the lower kinds of flesh, which embrace the Negro. Hence if it is criminal to give the Bible to dogs, it is criminal to give it to the Negro. If it is criminal to undertake to Christianize swine, it is criminal to undertake to Christianize the Negro. In these respects man can make no distinction between one animal and another. This prohibitory law applies with equal force to the mixed-bloods. They possess none of the spiritual creation, but are wholly animal. The heathen to whom the command that the gospel should be preached were the pure-blooded descendants of Adam who had lost their knowledge of the true God and of all religious worship, or had descended to idolatry."—Pages 166, 167.

Here our author does great violence to the words of our Savior in Matt. 7:6. We might as well say that Herod was a mixed-blood because Jesus called him a fox, and that the Pharisees and Sadducees were mixed-bloods because John the Baptist called them a generation of vipers (Matt. 3:7), as to say that the dog and the swine in our Savior's command, "Give not that which is holy unto dogs," etc., signifies the Negroes and mixed-bloods. There is nothing in the text that would justify such an interpretation; but the text itself shows that it will not admit it. Observe the reason assigned by our Savior why Christians are not to cast pearls before swine and holy things unto dogs—"lest they trample them under their feet, and turn again and rend you." These words form the key to this text. He refers to such men as are so filled with unbelief that they are almost entirely insusceptible to the gospel. Such persons are found among all races and classes of the human family.

They will stubbornly resist the gospel when it is preached unto them, and despite your efforts to lead them to Christ they will turn again and rend you; that is, seek to destroy both Christianity and its advocates. Such are the dogs and swine that Christian ministers are cautioned not to waste time with. But for Mr. Carroll to say that these devouring creatures are found only among the Negroes and mixed-bloods and that Jesus gave the injunction because such have no souls, is only indulging in that kind of presumption that is so common throughout his book.

But concerning the commission, that it was limited to the Caucasian race, I would say that the very words with which the Savior puts it forth refutes this idea. Observe how broad he makes it. "Go ye into all the world."—Mark 16:15. "Go ye therefore and teach all nations." If Mr. Carroll's theory be true these injunctions do not mean what they say. He tells us that none but the pure-blooded Caucasians are men and are included in the commission. He also tells us on pages 170, 171 of his book that the whites have disappeared from three of the five continents, and that the remnant of the white descendants are practically confined to portions of Europe and America. Therefore according to his theory the Savior did not mean what he said, that we should actually go into all the world, and teach all nations—He simply means that we should go to two of the continents and preach the gospel only to the Caucasians.

It would appear from the wording of the commission that our Savior foresaw the heresy of Mr. Carroll and put forth the commission in words that were well calculated to refute it. Mr. Carroll tells us that we should only carry the gospel to two of the continents, and Jesus tells us to carry it into all the world.

Mr. Carroll tells us that we need not bother with the Negroes of Africa, nor with the Laplanders, Finns, and Basques of Europe, nor with the Hindoos, Coreans, Chinese, Japanese, etc., of Asia, nor with the Australians, Malays, etc., of Oceanica, nor with the wild hunting tribes of North and South America, nor with the Mexicans, Peruvians, etc., because he says they are not included in the plan of salvation— and his say is all we have for that kind of doctrine— but Jesus puts his say up against Mr. Carroll's say and tells us to go and teach all nations. Mr. Carroll must not deny that all these classes of people whom he tells us are not men constitute nations, and therefore can not get around the fact that we are commanded to carry the gospel to them. And as these colored races inhabit such a large portion of the world it is im-

possible for us to obey our Savior's command, "Go ye
into all the world and preach,"except we preach the
gospel unto them; for Mr. Carroll himself tells us that
there are no Caucasians among them. But behold the
wisdom of Jesus in the framing of this commission.
He did not say Go into all the world and preach the
gospel to all men—that indeed would have been plain
enough—but he seems to have foreseen that a man by
the name of Carroll would arise in these days and tell
us that only Caucasians were men; therefore the commission was made to read, "Go ye into all the world
and preach the gospel unto every creature." This
implies that we are to preach the gospel unto every
creature who possesses reason and can be brought
under the influence of the gospel.

It might be well to mark here how the Revelator
puts forth his invitation to the sinners in Rev. 22:17
—"The Spirit and the bride say, Come. And let him
that heareth say, Come. And let him that is athirst,
Come. And whosoever will, let him take the water
of life freely." Yea, answers every Christian, Let
every soul from among the black and colored races
who heareth the gospel, come, and let every soul,
whether he be Caucasian, Malay, Mongolian, Negro,
or Indian, that is athirst, come. Let every soul of
every nationality who will, take the water of life

freely. How different the voice that is sounded forth from the lips of Mr. Carroll. It is as follows: Let him that heareth among the whites say, Come. And let him that is athirst among the whites, Come. And whosoever will, if he is white, let him take of the water of life freely.

I might call the reader's attention also to a prophecy by Isaiah which shows how universal the call of the gospel is. "Look unto me, and be ye saved, all the ends of the earth: for I am God, and there is none else."—Isa. 45:22. If Mr. Carroll had written this prophecy it would have read as follows: "Look unto me, and be ye saved, all ye remnants of the whites in Europe and America." What Christian would not prefer the Bible as it is to Mr. Carroll's revisions? "All ye ends of the earth" takes in Malays, Mongolians, Negroes, and Indians, as well as Caucasians. We can not interpret it sensibly in any other light, because the whites are not dwelling in all the ends of the earth.

Mr. Carroll's doctrine requires the little parenthesis "if you are white" inserted in all the invitations to the sinner to come to Christ that are found in the Bible. Let us fix a few of them up that way and see how they sound. "Look unto me, and be ye saved, all ye ends of the earth—if you are white."—Isa. 45:

22. "Come unto me, all ye that labor and are heavy laden—if ye are white."—Matt. 11:28. "Let him that is athirst,—if he is white—come. And whosoever will, if he is white, let him take the water of life freely."—Rev. 22:17. "I will give unto him that is athirst, if he is white, of the fountain of the water of life freely."—Rev. 21:6. "Ho, every one that thirsteth, come ye, if ye are white, to the waters, and he that hath no money; come ye,—if ye are white— buy, and eat; yea, come, buy wine and milk without money and without price."—Isa. 55.1. "Whosoever drinketh of the water that I shall give him—if he is white—shall never thirst; but the water that I shall give him—if he is white—shall be in him a well of water springing up into everlasting life."—Jno. 4:14. "I am the bread of life: he that cometh to me—if he is white—shall never hunger; and he that believeth on me—if he is white—shall never thirst."—Jno. 6:35. "If any man eat of this bread,—if he is white —he shall live forever."—Jno. 6:51. "If any— white—man thirst, let him come unto me, and drink. He that believeth on me,—if he is white—as the scrip- ture hath said, out of his belly shall flow rivers of living water."—Jno. 7:37, 38. "Who will have all —white—men to be saved and to come to a knowledge of the truth."—1 Tim. 2:4. "The Lord is not slack

concerning his promise, as some men count slackness, but is long-suffering to usward, not willing that any —white—man should perish, but that all—white—men should come to repentance."—2 Pet. 3:9.

Mr. Carroll may call this ridicule, but it is only an exhibition of his theory. I prefer to use the good old Bible as it is and to leave out all the interpolations which his doctrine requires. I prefer to obey our Savior and go forth and teach all nations regardless of their color. I prefer also to go into all the world and preach the gospel and not confine myself to a few places in two continents. If I were to accept Mr. Carroll's doctrine I would not know how to carry it out perfectly; for I would have no way of telling exactly who has a soul.

He tells us that in the beginning God created a black beast—the Negro—and the white man, and that amalgamation of these two species has caused the various colors in the world. He tells us also that the Negro has no soul, and that none of the crosses between him and man possess souls. According to his doctrine if there is the thousandth part of this black beast (?) in a man, he possesses no soul. But I am certain it would require the most scrutinizing scientific investigations to tell who had and who had not souls. How am I to tell that in my ancestors, the Germans, far back in their remote antiquity there has not been some crossing with some of the dark-skinned tribes? How then am I to know that I am a man and possess a soul? How does Mr. Carroll know that there has not been in the remote past such an amalgamation in his ancestry that might be so nearly bred out that at this day it would not be discernible? I would like to have Mr. Carroll prove to us, according to his theory, that he is a man and has a soul, so that I being a minister of the gospel, may know whether I am to preach the gospel unto him. I defy him according to his theory to prove anybody to be of pure Adamic stock—a man possessing a soul, and included in the gospel invitations. If he attempts to prove that he is a man by his theory he will find he has undertaken a tremendous job. It will require at least another fifteen years to complete the task. The only way to avoid these difficulties is to ignore entirely the theory of Mr. Carroll, and we are not making a sacrifice when we do so; because his entire theory is built upon the hypothesis that the Negro is a beast. He has twisted the scriptures in a remarkable manner in order to wedge his assumed position into the holy Bible, but has failed in every attempt; and he comes out just where he started in—with an empty hypothesis.

Continuing to argue the limit upon the commission, Mr. Carroll says: "The Savior's decree, 'Go ye into all the world and preach the gospel to every creature' —that is, to every creature for whom it was designed —was fully executed. Paul says that in his day the gospel was preached to every creature which was under heaven. Col. 1:23. This sweeping statement of the learned apostle was either true or false. We accept it as unquestionably true. The gospel reached all for whom it was intended, yet it was not preached to the wild tribes of the Negroes and mixed-bloods of Africa, nor to the Laplanders, Finns, and Basques of Europe, nor to the Hindoos, Coreans, Chinese, Japanese, etc., of Asia, nor to the Australians, Malays, etc., of Oceanica, nor to the wild hunting tribes of North and South America, nor to the Mexicans, Peruvians, etc., etc., and no well informed man or woman will say that it was. This being true, it follows that Paul either misrepresented the facts when he said that in his day the gospel was preached to every creature which is under heaven, or the Negroes, Hindoos, Chinese, Malays, Indians, Basques, etc., are not included in the plan of salvation. It the gospel as published by the primitive church was confined to the pure white and was not preached to the Negro and the so-called brown, red, and yellow races of the

earth, where does the modern church obtain its
authority to extend it to them?"—Pages 167, 168.

No, Mr. Carroll, Paul did not misrepresent facts in
Col. 1:23, neither is it true that the nations who had not
heard the gospel prior to the time Paul uttered these
words are not included in the plan of salvation. You
simply misunderstand Paul, that is all. Paul did not
mean to teach that every creature who was of the
stock of Adam had heard the gospel. Such an idea is
not contained in the original. *En pase te ktisei* should
be translated "in all the creation," instead of "to
every creature," as in the Authorized Version. The
text therefore should read: "Which was proclaimed in
all the creation under heaven." It is so rendered in
substance in the following translations: Revised
Version, Catholic Bible, Conybeare and Howson,
Bible Union, Rotherham, and Syriac Version.

Paul conveyed about the same idea in other places.
In verse six of the same chapter, speaking of the
spread of the gospel, he says: "Which has come unto
you, as it has in all the world." Also in Rom. 10:18
he says: "But I say, Have they not heard? Yes
verily, their sound went into all the earth, and their
words unto the ends of the world." These expressions simply mean that the gospel was spread pretty
well over the then-known world. They had carried

the gospel as far as Spain (Paul himself preached in that country), and Spain is situated in what was then known as the western end of the world. They carried the gospel also very far to the East. Hippollytus tells us that the apostle Bartholomew carried the gospel into India, and that Thomas preached to the Parthians, Medes, Persians, Hyrcanians, Bactrians, and Margians. India lies on another end of the world as known to the apostle Paul. So he was justifiable in his saying that their words went into all the earth and unto the ends of the world. But our author is mistaken when he thinks that the early Christians carried the gospel unto all the Caucasians, and that they did not carry it unto any of the other races. It is quite certain that a number of the Caucasian races of Europe never heard the gospel preached in the days of the apostles. This is true especially of England, Ireland, and Germany. It is quite clear in history that Germany did not receive the gospel until the third century, and certain parts of Germany not before the fifth. Ireland was converted to Christianity by the Irish apostle Patrick in the fifth century. Among the dark-skinned nations that received the gospel in an early day may be mentioned the various tribes of Arabia, Egypt, Ethiopia, and beyond doubt also Lybia. So we are not to understand Paul's

words in Col. 1:23 in the absolute sense that our
author takes them.

The teachings of Christ will warrant our saying that
the commission which enjoined Christian ministers to
go into all the world and preach the gospel unto every
nation has not yet been accomplished; because Jesus
tells us plainly in Matt. 24:14—"And this gospel of
the kingdom shall be preached in all the world for a
witness unto all nations, and then shall the end come."
The end has not yet come, therefore the gospel has not
yet been preached in all the world for a witness unto
all nations; but it is moving upon its circuit. Christianity was revealed in western Asia. Its principal
course since its birth has been westward. It moved
across Europe and northern Africa, then to the isles
of the sea, then to the American continent, then to
the islands of the Pacific, and it finally struck eastern
Asia—Japan, China, and India. It has yet to travel
across the Asiatic continent, when its circuit will have
been completed. Surely, according to the words of
our Savior, the end must then come.

Our author makes the destruction of amalgamation
the principal, if not the sole, mission of Christ into
this world, as the following quotations from his book
will show. "The New Testament abounds with
denunciations of fornication, and fornicators, which

indicates that fornication was prevalent in the days
of the Savior and that, like the prophets who preceded
him, his mission was to break up this wicked, destructive practice and the social, political, and religious
equality with the Negro which inevitably leads to it,
and to restore the relation of master and servant
which God established between man and the Negro in
the creation."—Page 212. "The drift of Bible history
from the creation to the birth of the Savior clearly
indicates that he came to destory man's social,
political, and religious equality with the Negro and
the mixed-bloods and the amalgamation to which
these crimes inevitably lead, and to build the barriers
which God erected in the creation between man and
the ape."—Page 269.

These sayings of Mr. Carroll grossly misrepresent
the doctrine of the New Testament. In all the teachings of our Savior and in all the writings of the
apostles that have come down to us there is not a
fragment of evidence that a distinction between white
and colored races—so far as political, religious, and
social rights are concerned—formed any part of the
doctrine of Christ. But contrariwise, it is on record
that Christianity destroys the distinctions that existed
between various classes of the human family at the
time our Savior appeared. Equality is a prominent

doctrine of the New Testament.   Christ found a
great distinction existing in the Jewish nation between
clergy and laity, but he destroyed that and instituted
in his church a common equality, saying to his
disciples, "Be not ye called Rabbi; for one is your
Master, even Christ; and all ye are brethren."—Matt.
23:8.   "Neither be ye called masters; for one is your
Master, even Christ."—Ver. 10.

Jesus also at his appearance found among the Jews,
as well as among other nations, a distinction between
male and female that deprived the female of her rights
and liberties.   Also he found a great prejudice
existing between various nations, especially between
the Jews and all other nations.   But he has inspired
his apostle Paul to tell us that his doctrine destroys
all these distinctions.   "For as many of you as have
been baptized into Christ have put on Christ.   There
is neither Jew nor Greek, there is neither bond nor
free, there is neither male nor female: for ye are all
one in Christ Jesus."—Gal. 3:27, 28.   "For there is
no difference between the Jew and the Greek: for the
same Lord over all is rich unto all that call upon him.
For whosoever shall call upon the name of the Lord
shall be saved."—Rom. 10:12, 13.   "Where there is
neither Greek nor Jew, circumcision nor uncircumci-
sion, Barbarian, Scythian, bond nor free: but Christ is
all and in all."—Col. 3:11.

The doctrine set forth in these texts, rather than build up slavery, would destroy it from among a Christian people; and beyond doubt this very doctrine has destroyed it in the civilized world, and Christian people have found out that slavery only belongs to heathenism, and not to civilization nor Christianity. Do these scriptures sound as though the doctrine of Mr. Carroll is true, that Christ came to destroy the social, political, and religious equality between the white and black races? The reader can see that our author has built up this idea also upon false conceptions, and misunderstandings of the gospel of Christ. The colored people, according to the gospel, have equal rights, socially, politically, and religiously, with the white race, and none but ignorant and prejudiced minds think of taking these, their privileges, from them. But we often hear the enemies of the colored race affirm that equality with the colored races means a mixture of blood. This is not at all necessary. I am sure that I can and do recognize the colored races as entitled to equal rights with myself, yet I could not think of advocating marriages with them; for there is entirely too great a contrast between the races for happiness to grow out of such a union. But the fact that I do not believe in marriages with them is no reason why I should look upon them as beasts

and mixed-blooded apes.   No, I am sure I do not.   I
will treat them as kindly as I will the white race.   And
how can I exemplify the gospel of Jesus Christ except
I do?

I will now observe that Mr. Carroll charges the death
of Christ exclusively to amalgamation of the whites
with the Negroes, and states plainly that but for this
amalgamation it would not have been necessary for
Jesus Christ to have died.   He sets forth the parable
of the householder as recorded in the twenty-first
chapter of Matthew.   That the reader may have this
parable before him, I will quote it before I insert his
comment upon the same.

"Hear another parable   There was a certain householder, which planted a vineyard, and hedged it round
about, and digged a wine-press in it, and built a
tower, and let it out to husbandmen, and went into a
far country: and when the time of the fruit drew
near, he sent his servants to the husbandmen, that
they might receive the fruits of it.   And the husbandmen took his servants, and beat one, and killed
another, and stoned another.   Again, he sent other
servants more than the first: and they did unto them
likewise.   But last of all he sent unto them his son,
saying, They will reverence my son.   But when the
husbandmen saw the son, they said among themselves,

This is the heir: come, let us kill him, and let us seize on his inheritance. And they caught him, and cast him out of the vineyard, and slew him. When the lord therefore of the vineyard cometh, what will he do unto these husbandmen? They say unto him, He will miserably destroy those wicked men, and will let out his vineyard unto other husbandmen, which shall render him the fruits in their seasons.

"Jesus saith unto them, Did ye never read in the scriptures, The stone which the builders rejected, the same is become the head of the corner: this is the Lord's doing, and it is marvelous in our eyes? Therefore say I unto you, The kingdom of God shall be taken from you, and given to a nation bringing forth the fruits thereof. And whosoever shall fall on this stone shall be broken: but on whomsoever it shall fall, it will grind him to powder. And when the chief priests and Pharisees had heard his parables, they perceived that he spake of them. But when they sought to lay hands on him, they feared the multitude, because they took him for a prophet." — Matt. 21:33-46.

Our author's comment upon this parable is as follows: "In this parable with God as the householder, the earth the vineyard, souls the fruit, the prophets the servants, Jesus Christ the son and heir,

we have an exact illustration of Bible history from the
creation to the crucifixion. This parable teaches (1)
that the earth is the Lord's, that God let it out to
man, whom he desired should be fruitful and multiply,
and by a life of obedience would fit their souls for the
companionship of the blest, and thus increase the
population of heaven. But man violated the law of
God and condescended to social equality with the
Negro, and this led to amalgamation; and, as we have
shown, the amalgamated progeny of man and the
Negro produces no souls. And when God sent his
prophets to insist that they abandon their wicked
course and confine their marriage relations to the
Adamic family, and thus be able to give the Lord his
dues, they beat, and stoned, and killed them. God
then sent other prophets time and again, and they
did unto them likewise. (2) It teaches that the
second prophet and each succeeding prophet came for
the same purpose as did the first, and that the mission
of the son was identically the same as that of the
prophets who preceded him and that it shared the
same fate. (3) It teaches that if the first prophet
had succeeded in his mission there would have been
no necessity for sending a second, nor any subsequent
prophet, neither would it have been necessary to send
the son; had the Lord received his dues he would have

been satisfied. (4) It teaches the doctrine that it was a part of the general plan that the Savior should come and be sacrificed, and that everything pointed to his coming and sacrifice, is a mistake growing out of our failure to understand the nature of his mission and that of the prophets who preceded him. On the contrary, every effort was made to do away with the necessity of his coming and sacrifice. It was the last resort."—Pages 247-249.

Mr. Carroll, you do greatly err through your misunderstanding of the scriptures and of the plan of salvation. You have a wrong conception of this parable. The vineyard in this parable does not refer, as you say, to the earth, but represents the kingdom of God, which he established in Israel in the Old Testament dispensation. Jesus himself explained this parable in this light in his conversation with the Jews at the conclusion of the parable, which was as follows: "When the Lord therefore of the vineyard cometh, what will he do unto those husbandmen? They [Jews] say unto him, He will miserably destroy those wicked men, and will let out his vineyard unto other husbandmen, which shall render him the fruits in their seasons. Jesus saith unto them, Did ye never read in the scriptures, The stone which the builders rejected, the same is become the head of the corner: this is the Lord's doing, and it is marvelous in our

eyes? Therefore say I unto you, The kingdom of God
shall be taken from you, and given to a nation bringing
forth the fruits thereof."

Observe how Jesus used the words vineyard and
kingdom of God interchangeably. He says the householder planted a vineyard. The Jews said in answer
to his question, that the householder would "let out
his vineyard unto other husbandmen, which shall
render him the fruits in their seasons." Then Jesus
said, "Therefore say I unto you, The kingdom of God
shall be taken from you and given to a nation bringing
forth the fruits thereof." This prophecy of Jesus
came true when the kingdom of God departed from
the Jewish nation and was transferred to the Gentile
nations. So our author is mistaken about this parable
containing a history of the entire world back to the
creation. It can not possibly be traced further back
than the time of Abraham. The destruction of the
husbandmen and the burning of their city referred to
in the parable occurred at the destruction of Jerusalem and the dispersion of the Jews in A. D. 70. The
fruits of the vineyard signify righteousness and obedience to God. This we may understand by considering
the nature of the fruit the kingdom of God bears since
it has come over to the Gentiles. "For the kingdom
of God is not meat and drink, but righteousness, and
peace, and joy in the Holy Ghost."—Rom. 14:17.

"But the fruit of the Spirit is love, joy, peace, long-suffering, gentleness, goodness, faith, meekness, temperance."—Gal. 5:22, 23.   "For the fruit of the Spirit is in all goodness and righteousness and truth; proving what is acceptable unto the Lord."—Eph. 5: 9, 10.   These texts prove unquestionably that the fruit of the kingdom of God among the Gentiles is righteous living.   The fruit therefore which the kingdom of God bore when it was confined to Israel must have been fruit of the some kind, though not such an abundant crop as it bears in the gospel dispensation.   You see, reader, that Mr. Carroll's theory, that the fruit of the vineyard is pure, white-blooded children, is false.

In the conclusion of this chapter I want to show how badly mistaken our author is in his theory that it was not a part of the general plan that the Savior should come and be sacrificed.   He says: "This idea has grown out of our failure to understand the nature of his mission and that of the prophets who preceded him."   Then, my friends, the apostles of Christ failed to understand the nature of his mission and that of the prophets; because they teach that it was a part of the general plan of salvation that Christ should die for the salvation of the world.   The apostle John evidently understood that Christ was a "Lamb slain from the foundation of the world."—Rev. 13:8. *Peter also* evidently understood that it was a part of

the general plan of salvation that Christ should die;
for he says, "Forasmuch as ye know that ye were
not redeemed with corruptible things, as of silver and
gold, from your vain conversation received by tradition from your fathers; but with the precious blood of
Christ, as of a lamb without blemish and without
spot: who verily was foreordained before the foundation of the world, but was manifest in these last times
for you."—1 Pet. 1:18-20.   The foundation of the
world mentioned here by Peter doubtless refers to the
foundation of the new world which Peter reckons
began with Noah, in whose days he shows that a
new world was started.   2 Pet. 3:6, 7.   See also 1
Pet. 2:5.   So Peter's expression concerning Christ's
death, that it was foreordained before the foundation
of the world, will take us back to the foundation of
the old world when Adam and Eve transgressed God's
commands and fell into sin.   This harmonizes with
the Revelator's words in Rev. 13:8.

It is a misunderstanding of the fall as well as of the
doctrine of the atonement that causes Mr. Carroll to
say that the death of Christ could have been avoided
but for the sin of amalgamation with the Negroes.
When Adam had fallen into sin he stained with sin
the germ of every human being, because they were all
in his loins; hence the entire human family were
doomed to be born into the world in a depraved con-

dition. See Rom. 5:12-21. When man had once fallen into sin he could not by his own power regain his former condition of holiness, hence the necessity of an atonement. In that sinful condition man was under the penalty for sin, namely, death. Gen. 2:17; Eze. 18:4. This penalty must by all means be paid. By atonement it is understood that God accepts the death of another instead of that of the offender. It is in this light that we are to view the death of Christ. Soon after the fall, man began to offer animals in sacrifice to God; but the animals he offered were not perfect atonements, as they were not the equal of man, the offender. The offering of the blood of Christ is a perfect sacrifice, because it is the blood both of the divine and human being, both of the offended and the offender. Such must produce a perfect reconciliation between the divine and the human beings and purchase perfect favor for the latter in the sight of the former.

The offerings under the Old Testament were neither divine nor human,—the blood of lower animals—hence they could not produce a perfect reconciliation between God and man. Since, therefore, the blood of animals could not redeem men, and the blood of one man could not redeem another, as all men were in a like sinful condition, there was no avoiding the death of Christ to atone for man. If there had been one man in the world who was himself free from sin, he

could have redeemed one man by dying in his stead;
but he must have died eternally, since the penalty
of sin is eternal death.   It would have taken as many
holy men as there were sinful men to have redeemed
the human family.   But since there were no holy men,
men were entirely unredeemable without the sacrifice
of the Son of God.   Jesus being holy and being divine
could make a perfect atonement for man, nor need he
suffer eternally to pay the eternal death penalty for
man.   An infinite being as he is can pay an infinite
death penalty for an infinite number of people instanta-
neously.   This he did when he gave up the ghost.
Surely no man who understands the condition of the
human family under the fall and the necessity for an
atonement, could say, as Mr. Carroll has, that it was
not in the general plan of God that the Messiah
should die, but amalgamation with Negroes made it a
necessity.

THE IMAGE OF GOD.

ANOTHER argument brought forth by Mr. Carroll to prove that the Negro is not a man, is based upon the scriptural narrative that man was created in the image of God. The following quotations from his book explain his argument. "We must repudiate this atheistic theory that man is a highly developed species of ape and accept the scriptural teaching that man is a distinct creation in the image of God."— Page 311. "This being true, it follows that if the white was created in the image of God, then the Negro was made after some other image; and a glance at the Negro indicates the model. His very appearance suggests the ape."—Page 90. "Eve, fresh from the hands of her Creator, presented in her physical, mental, and spiritual organisms the most sublime specimen of that lovely sex upon whose fair brow is stamped the image of God."—Page 97.

The above words of Mr. Carroll betray a very imperfect understanding of the scriptures. He believes that God is white, and that therefore the

white man is created in his image; and that the
Negro, because he is black, is not created in the image
of God.   To say that the image of God in which man
was created is complexion or even features, betrays
the greatest ignorance of the Bible. If the image of
God is complexion and features, as our author
believes, then man has never lost it.   But since the
scriptures teach that in the fall man fell from the
image of God in which he was created, it is evident
that "the image of God" has no reference to features
and complexion.   To prove that man has fallen from
the image of God, I have but to prove that this image
is restored to man when he is redeemed in Christ
Jesus.   This idea is set forth in the epistles of St.
Paul, from which I quote. "Lie not one to another,
seeing that ye have put off the old man with his
deeds; and have put on the new man, which is renewed
in knowledge after the image of him that created
him."—Col. :9, 10.   The old man mentioned here
is Adam; the new man is Christ.   By putting off the
old man is meant deliverance from the effects of
Adam's sin, which is the nature and life of sin; and
by putting on the new man is meant the obtaining of
the nature and life of Christ. · And mark, he tells us
this new man is "renewed in knowledge after the
image of him that created him." Now we are certain
that when we obtain salvation through the blood of

Christ there is no change wrought in our features nor
in our complexion. Neither in the first nor second
work of grace is there such a change wrought in us.
The change is entirely a moral one; hence the image
of God that is restored to us in full salvation must be
a moral image. If this image is restored to us in full
salvation, it is evident that it had been lost in the fall;
and if in the fall man lost the image of God in which
he was created, it is evident that it was not complexion
and features, as our author supposes, but the moral
nature of God.

The image of God restored to us when we are
sanctified wholly is explained in Eph. 4:22-24. "That
ye put off concerning the former conversation the old
man, which is corrupt according to the deceitful lusts;
and be renewed in the spirit of your mind; and that
ye put on the new man, which after God [in the image
of God] is created in righteousness and true holiness."
A careful comparison of this text with Col. 3:10 shows
that the image of God restored to us in Christ is righteousness and true holiness. If God's image of righteousness and true holiness is restored to us in Christ,
it was this image of righteousness and true holiness
that we lost in Adam; the same image of righteousness
and true holiness in which Adam and Eve were
created. The expression "image of God" has reference to nothing else.

Solomon doubtless understood the image of God in
this light; because he says in Eccl. 7:29—"Lo, this
only have I found, that God hath made man upright;
but they have sought out many inventions." How
did Solomon discover that God had made man upright,
but by the inspired writings that preceded him? Since
there is nothing in the inspired writings antedating
Solomon to show that man was created upright, except
the little phrase "in the image of God," he must have
obtained this information from that very thing.

Soon after Adam had fallen from the image of God
by committing sin, he begat children: but of none of
these children is it written that "Adam begat a son
in the image of God." No; Adam was not in the
image of God any longer. Ne was no longer a holy
being, but a sinful being; hence he could not beget
children in the image of God in which he had been
created. But we are told that "Adam lived an
hundred and thirty years, and begat a son in his own
likeness, after his image; and called his name Seth."
—Gen. 5:3. Every human being has been begotten
in the image of Adam, that is, in a sinful condition;
none have come into the word in the image of God,
except Adam and Eve our first parents, and Christ,
who had no earthly father. Ile (Christ) coming in
the image of God to be our Savior, restores us by his
precious blood to this same image of righteousness

and holiness. The apostle Paul, speaking of this transformation into God's image by the blood of Christ, says: "But we all, with open face beholding as in a glass the glory of the Lord, are changed into the same image from glory to glory even as by the Spirit of the Lord."—2 Cor. 3:18.

The falling of the entire human family from the image of God by the sin of Adam is expressed by Paul as follows: "By one man sin entered into the world." —Rom. 5:12. "Through the offense of one many be dead."—Ver. 15. "The judgment was by one to condemnation."—Ver. 16. "By one man's offense death reigned by one."—Ver. 17. "By the offense of one judgment came upon all men to condemnation."— Ver. 18. "By one man's disobedience many were made sinners."—Ver. 19. The one man mentioned in these verses was Adam, who is reckoned the cause of the sinful condition of the entire human family; hence every child that comes into this world possesses a depraved nature. It is not in a guilty condition because of its ignorance of God's law, as Paul teaches in the seventh chapter of Romans, from which I quote. "For I was alive without the law once: but when the commandment came, sin revived, and I died. And the commandment, which was ordained to life, I found to be unto death. For sin, taking occasion by the commandment, deceived me, and by it slew me."—

Verses 9-11. Paul is here describing the infantile
state by giving us his own experience. He testifies
that he was alive without the law once, but when the
commandment came, sin revived, and he died. This
must have been when he was too young to comprehend
God's law; for in no other period of his life was he
without it. When a knowledge of God's law came to
him, he says, sin, which had been conceived and born
in his heart (Ps. 51:5), revived, and he died: that is,
he committed sin and died a spiritual death "in tres-
passes and in sins."—Eph. 2:1. Such a change takes
place in every child when he arrives at a knowledge of
good and evil. This period in life we are accustomed
to call the age of accountability. After he passes the
age of accountability and commits actual sin before
God, he is a guilty sinner and will be lost without
repentance. Had he died prior to this age he would
have been passive in the blood of Christ, and sanctified
unconditionally and taken home to glory, free from
inherited sin. But to die in the condition he has now
fallen into is to be eternally banished from the
presence of God.

When the soul who has thus fallen into actual sin
comes to Christ, repents of his sins, and receives the new
birth, he is forgiven by God of all the sins he has committed since he passed the age of accountability, and
is restored to his infantile innocence. But the sinful

nature he inherited from Adam still remains in his heart, and is manifest by way of anger, jealousy, pride, etc. When he comes to God for the second work of grace and receives the baptism of the Holy Ghost, which destroys in him that inherent depraved nature, he is fully restored to God's image of righteousness and true holiness. Such is the redemption of man.

Having now seen that the image of God is righteousness and true holiness, Mr. Carroll's argument against the Negro being a man, which he bases upon the scriptural narrative that man was created in the image of God, is entirely refuted. As to man's complexion at the time of his creation, I am sure it is impossible to prove what it was. I could not prove that Adam was a white man, and I do not believe Mr. Carroll can; he has not done so in any part of his book, and I do not believe it can be proved, although he may have been. The complexion or the features of man, whatever they may be, is no barrier to his possessing the image of God ("righteousness and true holiness"). The poor Negro can have the image of God restored to his nature the same as the Caucasian. I am sure that I have seen some of them in this redeemed condition. Although he is dark complected, I am able by the grace of God to recognize him as my *full* brother in Christ, and to love him as the word of

God requires us to love our brethren.   I have always
considered when coming in contact with those who
would set aside a man because he is black on the
outside, that the inward condition of the rejecter
resembled very much the outward appearance of the
rejected.

SCIENTIFIC EVIDENCES.

MR. CARROLL attempts to build up his theory, that the Negro is a beast, upon scientific as well as scriptural evidences. He holds that science makes the Negro to be a beast. But he denounces in strongest terms the theory of evolution. A glance however at that part of his book which relates to scientific evidence reveals the fact that although he is an enemy of evolution his scientific arguments are derived from evolution sources. Hartman, Huxley, Haeckel, Darwin, and Winchell are infidels in his estimation, because they are evolutionists; yet it is to these and other advocates of evolution that he resorts for his proofs that the Negro is related to the ape family. His quotations from scientists are almost exclusively from evolution authors. If we should cancel from his book the citations from evolution authors, there would be practically nothing left of a scientific nature. So if he does have but little confidence in the doctrine of evolution, he must have a deal of confidence in those who hold to that theory. Not only does he quote from evolution authors, but he bases his theory upon evolution doctrines. He uses at least two noted doctrines of the evolutionists: (1) that lower animals possess the same mind that man possesses; (2) the doctrine of outward relation between the various kinds of animals. Evolutionists, who try to account for the existence of this world and all it contains by a process of natural generation rather than an act of creation on the part of God, are compelled to advocate the doctrine that animal mind is the same in essence as the human mind, to avoid the creation of a new element when the human species evolved (?) from those below them.

The outward relation existing between the various kinds of animals is used by evolutionists in proof of the theory that all the higher orders evolved from the lower. This theory Mr. Carroll rightly calls infidelity, and he has no use for such a theory; but he can take the writings of these infidels as proof of his own erroneous theory. In this he makes a mistake, for two reasons; viz., (1) the writings of these skeptics are biased; and (2) these observations are based upon the outward rather than the inward relations that exist in the animal kingdom. If evolutionists had kept constantly before their view the inward relation that exists between certain kinds of animals, which separates them from other kinds, they never could have built up the theory of evolution.

An outward relation exists in the vegetable kingdom as universally as in the animal kingdom; hence the botanist can see a tie of relationship extending throughout the entire vegetable realm. He traces this relationship by taking a plant of one kind and studying it in comparison with a plant of a similar kind; then he can take that similar plant and study it in relation to another plant similar to it, then he can study the similarity of the third plant with a fourth plant, and so on until he traces the relationship through the entire vegetable kingdom. But when he has reached the last plant he has before him a plant that can not be compared with the plant from which he started his observations.

So can relationship be traced through the animal kingdom. A man and a horse look nothing at all alike, yet the scientist can see a relationship between them; but he has to go a long way around to trace that relationship. He has to single out the animal that looks the most like man. Between it and man he sees a similarity. Then he gets another animal that is nearest like that animal that is most similar to man, and he studies the relationship existing between them. Then he finds something similar to that third animal; and in that way he can find a relationship existing between the physical body

of the man and the horse. But if he puts the
horse up beside the man he will not see much re-
semblance. This distant route of outward relationship is traced by the evolutionist through the entire
animal kingdom, and to him it is a proof that man
evolved from the species below him. But such a
theory has never been proven, any more than the
theory that all the higher species of vegetables evolved
from the lower species. No examples of such evolu-
tions have come beneath the observations of men of
our time, neither are they upon record anywhere.

"On the first day of August, 1885, Prof. Geo. E.
Post, M. D., of the Syrian Mission, a gentleman of
superior scientific attainments, visited the great
British Museum; which, with its vast collection of
specimens, would probably be the best place in all the
world to find the 'missing links' and note the 'origin
of species,' as written in the rocky records of the
universe. There he found Mr. Etheridge, one of
the foremost of British experts. After Mr. Etheridge
had examined and named certain fossils which Dr.
Post had brought, and shown him the wonder of the
great collection, Dr. Post says, in a letter to a former
colleague, since printed in the New York Evangelist:
" 'I asked him whether after all, this was not the
working out of mind and Providence. He turned to

me with a clear, honest look into my eyes and replied, *"In all this great museum there is not a particle of evidence of transmutation of species.* Nine-tenths of the talk of evolutionists is sheer nonsense, not founded on observation and wholly unsupported by fact. Men adopt a theory and then strain their facts to support it. I read all their books, but they make no impression on my belief in the stability of species. Moreover, the talk of the great antiquity of man is of the same value. *There is no such thing as a fossil man.* Men are ready to regard you as a fool if you will not go with them in all their vagaries. But this Museum is full of proofs of the *utter falsity of their views."* ' " —From "Was Moses Mistaken? or Creation and Evolution," by H. L. Hastings.

So the doctrine of evolution, like every other theory opposed to divine revelation, is based solely upon the suppositions of skeptics.

The internal relation existing between certain families of the animal kingdom which serves as a protection against the infusion of foreign blood into their progenitors, is the strongest evidence against the orthodoxy of the theory of evolution. This internal relation exists in the germs of life. The closest ties of relationship, therefore, are those which are manifest in the process of procreation. Those animals which

.will breed true to each other are surely more closely related than those which are similar to each other in outward appearance only. As this tie of inward relationship does not extend through the entire animal kingdom nor the entire vegetable kingdom, the theory of evolution must be false. Had Mr. Carroll fixed his eyes upon this inward relationship rather than the outward relationship that is talked about so much among evolutionists, his book would have been something else and would not have been entitled "The Negro a Beast." This doctrine of internal relationship makes the Negro a man, and no scientist on earth can deny it; for he breeds true to the human family, and will not cross with anything outside of it.

But Mr. Carroll does not handle even the doctrine of outward relationship fairly, for it does not prove the Negro a beast. The science of zoology sees no distinction whatever between the Negro and the Caucasian; it views them both as man. The colors of the various races are not sufficient distinction to the zoologist to justify a division of the human family into species; hence we see man in the science of zoology as a single species *sapiens,* which is the only species of the genus *homo,* which is the only genus of the order *Bimana.* All the various species of every *genus* of apes are placed in the order *quadrumana* by the zoologist. So true science sees no similarity between any race of man and the apes, though Mr. Carroll unscrupulously states in several places in his book that science points to the Negro as the highest species of ape. This is a false assertion as the reader can see. The apes are all *quadrumana*, that is, four-handed animals; while man is *bimana*, that is, a two-handed animal. The following marked distinctions between man and the ape family are noted by the zoologist.

"There are marked physical peculiarities, however, which distinguish man from the other animals. Thus, the position of the spinal opening in the middle third of the base of the skull, thereby balancing the head and admitting an upright posture; the sigmoid S-curve of the vertebral column; the ability of opposing the well-developed thumb to the fingers; the shortened foot, the sole resting flat on the ground; the size and position of the great toe; the length of the arms, reaching half-way from the hip to the knees; the relatively great development of brain; the freedom of the anterior extremities from use in locomotion, and the consequent erect and biped position. In addition, man is the only mammal that truly walks; that is endowed with the power of speech; and that is cosmo-politan, readily adapting himself to extremes of heat and cold, and making his home in all parts of the globe.

"There are intellectual and moral features, moreover, which place man high above all other animals. The scope of his mind and the possibilities of an immortal soul, mark the rank of a being who is alone declared to have been created 'in the image of God.'

"Common Origin of Man.—While in the human race there is but a single species, zoologists are accustomed to speak of several very distinctly-marked varieties. In respect to the dividing lines of the commonly-enumerated five races, authors disagree. So that, although there are some differences of structure and great diversity in the texture of the skin and the character of the hair of mankind in various localities, yet in the same nation there are similar varieties; and as marked diversities have repeatedly been observed in a single species of the domestic animals. We therefore agree with Dr. Prichard 'that no other differences occur than may fairly be attributed to the differences of external circumstances; and hence it may safely be concluded that the different races are all members of the same family, and the offspring of one common stock.'"

Evolutionists acknowledge the zoological distinctions between man and the apes. They also acknowledge that

the various races, the blacks, browns, reds, and whites,
are all men and proceeded from one common origin, as
the following words of Darwin the noted evolutionist.
will show. "Although the existing races of man
differ in many respects, as in color, hair, shape of
skull, proportions of the body, etc., yet if their whole
organization be taken into consideration they are found
to resemble each other closely in a multitude of points.
Many of these points are of so unimportant or of so
singular a nature that it is extremely improbable that
they should have been independently acquired by
aboriginal distinct species or races. The same remark
holds good with an equal or greater force with respect
to the numerous points of mental similarity between
the most distinct races of men. . . . . Now when
naturalists observe a close agreement in numerous
small details of habits, tastes, and dispositions between
two or more domesticated races, or between nearly
allied natural forms, they use this fact as an argument
that all are descended from a common progenitor who
was thus endowed; and consequently they all should
be classed under the same species. The same argument may be applied with much force to the races of
man."—Descent of Man, Part 1, Chap. 7.

We should not, after reading the above words from
the pen of the man who originated the theory that man .

owes his existence to evolution, fail to see that evolutionists acknowledge the facts taught by the science of zoology, that all the five races are of one common origin.   From what source then does Mr. Carroll obtain his information that science classes the Negro with the apes.   He does not get it from the science of zoology, neither deos he get it from the evolutionists. He must get it from the imaginations of his own heart; and his science must be such as that which the apostle Paul denominates "science falsely so called."—1 Tim. 6:20. The only scientific characteristic of Mr. Carroll's book is the pointing out, by quotations from evolution authors, certain characteristics in the Negro which he says are similar to the apes.   But as all these characteristics may sometimes be found in Caucasians, we can not regard this as any proof of his theory, that the Negro is a beast.

But whence arise the variations existing between various classes of the human family that justify their division into separate races?   These distinctions beyond doubt are all due to the variations of nature. It was formerly believed that the various colors were due principally to climatic influences, but this theory is almost universally disbelieved to-day among the scientists, since we have so many examples of white and dark-skinned people living side by side for cen-

turies in the same latitude and longitude, hence sub-
jected to the same climatic influences. But that these
distinctions are due to variations in nature and that
the laws of procreation are capable of producing these
various races, is beyond doubt the most reasonable
theory.

It is not alone in the human family that we see
these distinct races.   We see them also in nearly all
the species of lower animals; as, for instance, in the
pigeon. We have at least 150 kinds of these domestic
birds, yet they all beyond doubt descended from one
original pair.   If we apply Mr. Carroll's theory to the
pigeons, we would then suppose that God in the beginning created a pair of black pigeons and a pair of
white pigeons, and that all the various colors and races
of pigeons are the products of crosses between these
two distinct kinds.   In the ox species also we see distinct varieties.   Now if we apply Mr. Carroll's theory
here, we would suppose that God in the beginning
created a pair of white oxen and a pair of black oxen,
and that all the other colors, the red, the brown, the
blue, the spotted, the speckled, and the striped oxen,
are all the result of crosses between these two original
species.   This of course would be a ridiculous theory
when applied to the oxen, but it is no more ridiculous
than when applied by Mr. Carroll to the human family.

Now we know that this theory can not be true in
regard to the oxen, for we know some things about
producing the various colors at will.   Jacob in his
time knew how to produce the kind of hair he wanted
on the calves, as we read in Gen. 30:37-42, which I
quote.

"And Jacob took him rods of green poplar, and of
the hazel and chestnut-tree; and pilled white strakes
in them, and made the white appear which was in the
rods.   And he set the rods which he had pilled before
the flocks in the gutters in the watering troughs when
the flocks came to drink, that they should conceive
when they came to drink.   And the flocks conceived
before the rods, and brought forth cattle ringstraked,
speckled, and spotted.   And Jacob did separate the
lambs, and set the faces of the flocks toward the ringstraked, and all the brown in the flock of Laban; and
he put his own flocks by themselves, and put them not
unto Laban's cattle.   And it came to pass, whensoever
the stronger cattle did conceive, that Jacob laid the
rods before the eyes of the cattle in the gutters, that
they might conceive among the rods.   But when the
cattle were feeble, he put them not in: so the feebler
were Laban's, and the stronger Jacob's."

Here it is recorded that ringstreaked, speckled and
spotted calves were produced by Jacob at his will.

The means he used were simply green poles peeled in stripes and specks and spots and laid before the cattle, where they could look upon them at the time of their conception. If streaks and specks and spots can be thus put upon calves by the laws of procreation, can not various colors be placed upon the skin of man by the laws of procreation in the human family? Our knowledge of the laws of procreation is sufficient proof to us that nature is capable of producing all the distinct varieties of mankind in the world to-day. We know beyond doubt that the laws of procreation can be so governed as to produce in a child any faculty at the will of the parents. Scientists hold that the best time for a mother to educate her child is while it remains within her womb; that she can then incline its mind in the direction she chooses. We know also that the laws of procreation are capable of deforming a child in almost any conceivable manner. I know a club-footed young man who was thus deformed by his mother entering too deeply in sympathy, before the birth of her child, with a club-footed boy whom she saw hobbling along the road. Out of sympathy for this child, another woman marked her son in the same manner. Many are the examples of similar deformities that have been brought about through the laws of procreation in the female. Sometimes children have borne the marks of strangers, even of other races, through a scare of the mother. Sometimes certain gestures of lower animals have been stamped upon children in the same manner. It is also a frequent thing to see children of a second husband who resembled the former husband. This is due to the remembrance of the former husband by the mother. If all these variations have been demonstrated to us, can we not easily believe that all the distinctions existing in the human family are due also to the variations of the laws of procreation?

But as regards color, I would say it is difficult to find two persons who are shaded exactly alike. In the same family we find blondes and brunettes, different colors of eyes, different colors of the hair, and variations of the features. They all proceeded from the same father and the same mother. Mr. Carroll can not account for these things by his theory of amalgamation. If these striking variations are seen in a single family, how distinct might they become in thousands of years. It is an easy matter for us to believe that nature has painted the various nations of the human family to suit herself.

I would further observe that among those who are called Caucasians there are no two nations that are of exactly the same color. This is true also of all the

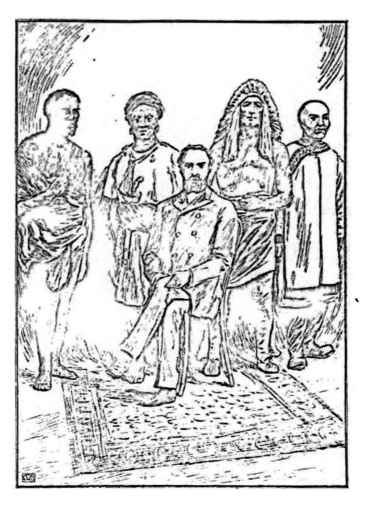

THE FIVE RACES.
AFRICAN, MALAY, CAUCASIAN, NORTH AMERICAN INDIAN, MONGLOIAN.

other races. Were we to denominate each separate color a race, we would have races innumerable. But if we lay aside color we find other distinct characteristics of certain nations that will serve as unanswerable proofs of the variations of nature; as, for instance, the hair of the Hottentot. It grows in small tufts, harsh and rather wiry, covering the scalp somewhat like the hard pellets of a shoe brush. If we were to acknowledge Mr. Carroll's theory to be true, that the various races sprang from amalgamation between the whites and blacks, we would still have to charge the peculiarity of the hair of the Hottentot to a variation of nature, since neither the black nor the white has any such hair. We might observe also that the Hottentot women have natural bussels. This same thing has been occasionally met in other nations, but among the Hottentots it is universal. Amalgamation between the whites and Negroes will not account for these humps upon the backs of the Hottentot women. We must acknowledge this to be another proof that nature varies.

Another striking evidence of the variation of nature that Mr. Carroll can not help seeing is found in the Bushmen of Africa. They are of remarkably small stature. Among 150 of their number measured by the traveler Barrow, the tallest man was four feet nine

inches, the tallest woman four feet four inches; and
they are not Negroes, but rather of a reddish brown
color similar to the Hottentots.   Now if Mr. Carroll's
theory were true and these little people are a cross
between the Negro and the white man, there would
be no way of accounting for their small stature but by
a variation of nature.

The hair of the Bushmen appears in small woolly
tufts with spaces between them, similar to that of the
Hottentots.   These things must be attributed to the
variations of nature.   There are many things that
might be mentioned which serve to prove the variations
of nature in the human family, but I have here only
attempted to mention such things as are capable of
proving the doctrine of variation, were the theory of
Mr. Carroll true.   If then we are driven independent
of the theory of our author to attribute certain
characteristics of some nations to the variations of
nature, how much more reasonable is the theory that
all the distinctive characteristics of the various races
and nations are due to the variations of nature, rather
than to crosses between two distinct species—white
man and black beast(?)?

Those who hold to the theory of Mr. Carroll might
raise the objection that the various freaks and variations of nature are not perpetuated.   But they *are*

perpetuated, generally. We are quite sure that the
tufts of hair on the Hottentot and Bushmen have been
perpetuated, likewise the natural bussels on the
Hottentot women. Since we must acknowledge these
characteristics to be freaks of nature, facts will compel
us to acknowledge also that these freaks have been perpetuated. There are many other examples of the per-
petuation of nature's variations that may be mentioned.
Some quotations from the Encyclopedia Brittanica,
article "Breeds and Breeding," will throw some light
upon this subject.

"Certain peculiarities have appeared only once or
twice in the history of the world, but have reappeared
in children or grandchildren of the individuals so
characterized. Thus Lambert, 'the porcupine man,'
whose skin was covered with warty projections which
were periodically moulted, had six children and two
grandsons similarly affected. The most striking cases
of inheritance have, as in this instance, been observed
in man; but the very existence of the numerous breeds
of domestic animals is clear evidence of the possibility
of the transmission of every kind of peculiarity. For
instance, it is believed that the varieties of the domestic
pigeon amount to at least 150, and these races differ
from each other in many ways and all breed true to
their kind. Some very curious peculiarities have been

perpetuated. . . . The fact that not even the most
complex combinations of qualities are capable of hereditary transmission is perhaps more forcibly brought
home by considering the monetary aspect of the art of
breedings than by the fullest collection of special
instances; as Mr. Herbert Spencer remarks: 'Excluding these inductions that have been so fully verified as
to rank with exact science, there are no inductions so
trustworthy as those which have undergone the mer-
cantile test.' . . . Not only are slight and gradual
changes inherited, but in some cases sudden and well-
marked variations are strongly transmitted. The case
of the Niata cattle is well known. A similar case is
recorded of a rabbit born with only one ear, from which
a breed was formed which steadily produced one-eared
rabbits. These remarkable cases of sudden and large
variation being inherited are closely allied to the still
more curious phenomenon of the inheritance of mutila-
tions. The most striking cases on record are those of
Brown-Sequard. In his experiments on the inheritance of artificially produced epilepsy, he found that
guinea-pigs, after having undergone section of the
sciatic nerve, often nibbled off portions of their hind
legs in consequence of the anæsthesia of those parts.
Now the offspring of these self-mutilated animals were
in thirteen cases born without toes, . . . In all cases

it must be remembered that the form and qualities which the offspring of an animal or plant will assume when fully developed are not solely dependant on the nature of the hereditary impetus with which it starts."

The facts set forth in these quotations are sufficient proofs to any teachable mind that the freaks and variations of nature may be hereditary. This hereditary law lies principally if not entirely in the female. It was the same hereditary law that caused Laban's calves to be spotted and ringstreaked when the mother looked upon the spotted and ringstreaked poles prepared by Jacob: that caused the children of the warty man to be similarly affected, by his wife looking upon his condition; also that caused the mutilated guinea-pigs to be born by the females who looked upon the self-mutilated males; and that caused the little one-eared rabbits to be born by the female who had the one-eared male rabbit for her companion. This being true, is it an unreasonable doctrine that many times nature has varied in the birth of children to the extent that their complexion differs from that of their parents, and that wives of men possessing these different features have begotten children of similar complexion by having those men continually before them? This is the only true scientific way to account for the many varieties of complexion and features in the human family.

Mr. Carroll's theory of amalgamation apart from the variations of nature can not account for all the various characteristics of the human family. A cross between blacks and whites produces mulattoes—nothing but mulattoes. It never develops the characteristics of the other races. The red, yellow, and brown races have characteristics peculiar to themselves which are not possessed by either the black or white races. These characteristics can not be accounted for by Mr. Carroll's theory of amalgamation. We must attribute them to the variations of nature. We have had amalgamation between whites and blacks in this country for two hundred years, yet this amalgamation has never produced any Chinese, nor any North American Indians, nor any Japanese—nothing but mulattoes. Since then we are compelled, independent of what light Mr. Carroll claims to reveal by his imaginary theory of amalgamation, to attribute so many distinctive characteristics to the variations of nature, we have just grounds, despite all he has said, to attribute all the variations of color, as well as other distinctions of the human family, to the variations of nature. I repeat what I said before: this is the only true scientific way to account for the various races of the human family.

HISTORIC EVIDENCES.

In all his book Mr. Carroll has not brought forth a single historic evidence of the truthfulness of his theory. He makes no reference to history except to deny some well-established facts. He dénies that the Negroes are descendants of Ham; he denies also that the Ethiopians were the descendants of Ham; and he even denies that the Ethiopians were Africans, but affirms that they were Asiatics and descendants of Shem. He even denies that the ancient Ethiopians were a colored race. A number of other plain facts in regard to the colored race which are well established in ancient history, he also flatly denies. In this chapter I shall show that the ancient Ethiopians were a colored race, that they were Africans, and that when the dispersion occurred at the confusion of tongues, the children of Ham settled in Africa. I shall also give some good scriptural reasons why the nations of Africa are colored.

I begin with the declaration of Paul in his famous sermon at Athens, recorded in the seventeenth chapter of Acts. "God that made the world and all things therein, seeing that he is Lord of heaven and earth, dwelleth not in temples made with hands; neither is worshiped with men's hands, as though he needed anything, seeing he giveth to all life, and breath, and all things; and hath made of one blood all nations of men for to dwell on all the face of the earth, and hath determined the times before appointed, and the bounds of their habitation."—Verses 24-26.

The "one blood" mentioned here out of which God has created all the nations of the earth was that which was contained in the family of Noah, all other human beings having been drowned in the flood. Out of this one family God has made all the nations of the earth; and this text tells us that he made all nations to dwell on all the face of the earth. That is, it was his intention that every part of the earth was to be peopled by some of these nations. It is a remarkable fact that every part of the earth is inhabited by nations of human beings. But Mr. Carroll tells us that there are no human beings except upon two continents; that three of the continents are entirely destitute of human beings. He can not well work his theory in here. Where the nations of black men live, should we recognize them as beasts, according to Mr. Carroll's theory, the nations created out of the one blood have never dwelt. But let us see.

If we turn to Gen. 11:9 we find it there written concerning the confusion and dispersion of the children of Noah as follows: "Go to, let us go down and there confound their language, that they may not understand one another's speech. So the Lord scattered them abroad from thence upon the face of all the earth: and they left off to build the city. Therefore is the name of it called Babel; because the Lord did there confound the language of all the earth: and from thence did the Lord scatter them abroad upon the face of all the earth." According to this the dispersion of the nations reached over the face of all the earth; therefore, we are to look for the descendants of Noah on the face of all the earth, and can not stake off certain continents or parts of continents and say these people are not the children of Noah because they are colored. Color has nothing to do with this historical fact. This history is based upon blood, and not upon color. The scripture does not say that God has made of one color all the nations of the earth for to dwell upon the face of all the earth; but it says, "God has made of one blood all the nations." Therefore, all the nations of all the continents, regardless of their color, are the true descendants of Noah, and we can not trace their ancestry to any other.

According to Paul's declaration in Acts 17, which I quoted above, it was God's intention that at the time of the flood the children of Noah should people the entire earth. This throws light upon the confusion of tongues; for if it was God's original plan that the children of Noah should be dispersed over all the earth. Nimrod's efforts to build a great tower and a city to hold the people together and prevent their dispersion, was directly opposed to the plan of God. This would bring the wrath of God upon them, and is doubtless the true cause of the confusion of tongues that the Lord sent upon them. God would have raised no objections to their use of a universal language, had they carried out his plan in peopling the entire world; but when they began to make use of the universality of their language to hold themselves in one locality and not subdue the entire earth according to his will, he destroyed the universality of their language, which rendered their dispersion a necessity.

As it may prove of interest to many readers, I will insert the account of the dispersion of the nations after the confusion of tongues that is given by Josephus in his renowned history entitled "Antiquities of the Jews." The quotation I am about to make from Josephus' history forms the fifth and part of the sixth chapters of the first book of his "Antiquities." I will quote the entire account, giving the chapter numbers and the headings, and marking the paragraphs just as they occur in Josephus' History, which will make the quotation very easily found in the works of Josephus.

CHAPTER V.

After what manner the posterity of Noah sent out colonies, and inhabited the whole earth.

1. After this they were dispersed abroad, on account of their languages, and went out by colonies everywhere; and each colony took possession of that land which they light upon, and unto which God led them; so that the whole continent was filled with them, both the inland and the maritime countries. There were some also who passed over the sea in ships and inhabited the islands: and some of those nations do still retain the denominations which were given them by their first founders; but some have lost them also, and some have only admitted certain changes in them, that they might be the more intelligible to the inhabitants. And they were the Greeks who became the authors of such mutations. For when in after ages they grew potent, they claimed to themselves the glory of antiquity; giving names to the nations that sounded well (in Greek) that they might be better understood among themselves; and setting agreeable forms of government over them, as if they were a people derived from themselves.

CHAPTER VI.

*How every nation was denominated from their first
inhabitants.*

1. Now they were the grandchildren of Noah, in hon-
or of whom names were imposed on the nations by those
that first seized upon them.   Japhet, the son of Noah,
had seven sons: they inhabited so, that, beginning at
the mountains Taurus and Amanus, they proceeded
along Asia as far as the river Tanais, and along Europe
to Cadiz; and settling themselves on the lands which
they light upon, which none had inhabited before, they
called the nations by their own names.   For Gomer
founded those whom the Greeks now call Galatians
[Galls], but were then called Gomerites.   Magog
founded those that from him were named Magogites,
but who are by the Greeks called Scythians.   Now as
to Javan and Madai, the sons of Japhet; from Madai
came the Madeans, who are called Medes by the
Greeks; but from Javan, Ionia, and all the Grecians,
are derived.   Thobel found the Thobelites, who are
now called Iberes; and the Moschcni were found by
Mosoch; now they are Cappadocians.   There is also
a mark of their ancient denomination still to be
shown; for there is even now among them a city called
Mazaca, which may inform those that are able to
understand, that so was the entire nation once called.

Thiras also called those whom he ruled over Thira-
sians; but the Greeks changed the name into Thra-
cians. And so many were the countries that had the
children of Japhet for their inhabitants. Of the three
sons of Gomer, Aschanax found the Aschanaxians,
who are now called by the Greeks Rheginians. So
did Riphath found the Riphcans, now called Paphla-
gonians; and the Thrugramma the Thrugrammeans,
who, as the Greeks resolved, were named Phrygians.
Of the three sons of Javan also, the son of Japhet,
Elisa gave name to the Eliseans, who were his subjects; they are now the Æolians. Tharsus to the
Tharsians, for so was Cilicia of old called; the sign of
which is this, that the noblest city they have, and a
metropolis also, is Tarsus, the *tau* being by change
put for the *theta*. Cethimus possessed the island
Cethima: it is now called Cyprus; and from that it
is that all islands, and the greatest part of the seacoasts,
are named Cethim by the Hebrews: and one city there
is in Cyprus that has been able to preserve its
denomination; it has been called Citius by those who
use the language of the Greeks, and has not, by the
use of that dialect, escaped the name of Cethim. And
so many nations have the children and grandchildren
of Japhet possessed. Now when I have premised
somewhat, which perhaps the Greeks do not know, I

will return and explain what I have omitted; for such
names are pronounced here after the manner of the
Greeks, to please my readers; for our own country
language does not so pronounce them: but the names
in all case are of one and the same ending; for the name
we here pronounce Noeas, is there Noah, and in every
case retains the same termination.

2. The children of Ham possessed the land from
Syria and Amanus, and the mountains of Libanus;
seizing upon all that was on its seacoasts, and as far
as the ocean, and keeping it as their own.   Some
indeed of its names are utterly vanished away; others
of them being changed, and another sound given them,
are hardly to be discovered; yet a few there are which
have kept their denominations entire.   For of the
four sons of Ham, time has not at all hurt the name
of Chus; for the Ethiopians over whom he reigned are
even at this day, both by themselves and by all men
in Asia, called Chusites.   The memory also of the
Mesraites is preserved in their name; for all we who
inhabit this country [of Judea] called Egypt Mestre,
and the Egyptians Mestreans.   Phut also was the
founder of Libya, and called the inhabitants Phutites,
from himself: there is also a river in the country of
the Moors which bears that name; whence it is that
we may see the greatest part of the Grecian historio-

graphers mention that river and the adjoining country
by the appellation of Phut: but the name it has now
has been by change given it from one of the sons of
Mesraim, who was called Lybyos.   We will inform you
presently what has been the occasion why it has been
called Africa also.   Canaan, the fourth son of Ham,
inhabited the country now called Judea, and called it
from his own name Canaan.   The children of these
[four] were these: Sabas, who founded the Sabeans;
Evilas, who founded the Evileans, who are called
Getuli; Sabathes founded the Sabathens, they are
now called by the Greeks Astaborans; Sabactas settled
the Sabactens; and Ragmus the Ragmeans; and he
had two sons, the one of whom, Judadas, settled the
Judadeans, a nation of the western Ethiopians, and
left them his name; as did Sabas to the Sabeans: but
Nimrod the son of Chus, staid and tyrannized at
Babylon, as we have already informed you.   Now all
the children of Mesraim, being eight in number, possessed the country from Gaza to Egypt, though it
retained the name of one only, the Philistim; for the
Greeks call part of that country Palestine.   As for
the rest, Ludieim, and Enemim, and Labim, who alone
inhabited in Libya, and called the country from himself, Nedim, and Phethrosim, and Chesloim, and
Cephthorim, we know nothing of them besides their

names; for the Ethiopic war, which we shall describe hereafter, was the cause that those cities were overthrown. The sons of Canaan were these: Sidonius, who also built a city of the same name; it is called by the Greeks Sidon: Amathus inhabited in Amathine, which is even now called Amathe by the inhabitants, although the Macedonians named it Epiphania from one of his posterity: Arudeus possessed the island Aradus: Aruças possessed Arce, which is in Libanus. But for the seven others [Eueus] Chetteus, Jebuseus, Amorreus, Gergesus, Eudeus, Sineus, Samareus, we have nothing in the sacred books but their names, for the Hebrews overthrew their cities; and their calamities came upon them on the occasion following.

3. Noah, when, after the deluge, the earth was resettled in its former condition, set about its cultivation; and when he had planted it with vines, and when the fruit was ripe, and he had gathered the grapes in their season, and the wine was ready for use, he offered sacrifice and feasted, and, being drunk, he fell asleep and lay naked in an unseemly manner. When his youngest son saw this, he came laughing and showed him to his brethren; but they covered their father's nakedness. And when Noah was made sensible of what had been done, he prayed for prosperity to his other sons; but for Ham, he did not curse him,

by reason of his nearness in blood, but cursed his posterity: and when the rest of them escaped that curse, God inflicted it on the children of Canaan. But as to these matters we shall speak more hereafter.

4. Shem, the third son of Noah, had five sons, who inhabited the land that began at Euphrates, and reached to the Indian Ocean. For Elam left behind him the Elamites, the ancestors of the Persians. Ashur lived at the city of Nineve; and named his subjects Assyrians, who became the most fortunate nation beyond others. Arphaxad named the Arphaxadites, who are now called Chaldeans. Aram had the Aramites, which the Greeks called Syrians; as Laud founded the Laudites, which are now called Lydians. Of the four sons of Aram, Uz found Trachonitis and Damascus: this country lies between Palestine and Celesyria. Ul founded Armenia; and Gather the Bactrians; and Mesa the Mesaneans; it is now called Charax Spasini. Sala was the son of Arphaxad; and his son was Heber, from whom they originally called the Jews Hebrews. Heber begat Joctan and Phaleg: he was called Phaleg because he was born at the dispersion of the nations to their several countries; for Phaleg among the Hebrews signifies division. Now Joctan, one of the sons of Heber, had these sons, Elmodad, Saleph, Asermoth, Jera, Adoram, Aizel, Decla, Ebal, Abimael, Sabeus,

Ophir, Euilat, and Jobab. These inhabited from
Cophen, an Indian river, and in part of Asia adjoining
to it. And this shall suffice concerning the sons of
Shem.

The reader will observe how clearly Josephus defines
the dispersion of the descendants of Noah. He even
gives in most instances the names of the countries that
were inhabited by the children of his three sons. If
we examine ancient geography we find that the nations
which sprang out of Japheth were nearly all located in
Europe; that the nations which sprang out of Shem
were located in Asia; and that the nations which
sprang out of Ham were nearly all located in Africa.
So it appears that the command of God dispersed the
three branches of the family of Noah in the direction
of the three grand divisions of the eastern continent.
Observe also that he makes it very clear when speaking
of certain descendants of Ham, that they settled in
the country that was called Africa.

Josephus promised that he would later in his book
inform us why this land has been called Africa. According to his promise, he explains this matter in the
15th chapter of the first book of his "Antiquities."
In this chapter he shows that the six sons of Abraham
by his second wife, Keturah (Gen. 25:1, 2), settled in

Arabia. One of these sons of Abraham, Midian, he
tells us, was the father of the Midianites, the nation
over which Gideon obtained the wonderful victory that
is recorded in the Bible. Josephus also tells us that
one of the sons of Midian, after they had settled in
Arabia, made war against the Lybians—a large nation
which had been founded by Phut, who was one of the
sons of Ham—and conquered them and brought them
under his control. This son of Midian was named
Ophron, or as it is otherwise pronounced, Apher.
From him this country of Lybia was named Africa,
which name afterwards extended to the entire grand
division now known as Africa.

Since we see that the children of Ham moved in
an African direction, we are to look for the Negro
tribes among them. So I will take up Ham and his
family and trace their names in the scriptures and
compare their signification with the history of the
nations that grew out of them, according to the
history of Josephus; and the reader will find that I
will have no trouble proving Ham to be the father of
colored races.

We are told in the Bible that Ham had four sons,
Cush, Mizraim, Phut, and Canaan. Josephus has
told us that Cush was the father of the Ethiopians,
who were formerly called Cushites; that Mizraim was

the father of the Egyptians, who were formerly called
Mizraimites; and that Phut was the father of the people of Lybia, who had formerly been called Phutites.
All these three nations we know to have been ancient
African nations.   Lybia was a large country that was
located in northern Africa and bordered on Egypt;
while Ethiopa was a large country of Africa that lay
south of Egypt.   Mr. Carroll says it was an Asiatic
country, but in this he is mistaken.   There is no doubt
that the Ethiopians had colonies in Arabia that were
located on the eastern coast of the Red Sea, but the
main country was located in Africa, as is evident by
the many references to it in ancient history, both
sacred and profane.   Ezek. 29:10 shows that it
bordered upon Egypt.   So we have at least three large
African nations—Lybians, Egyptians, and Ethiopians—
who descended from Ham.   Apart from the children of
Canaan, who settled principally in that part of western
Asia which afterwards became the Holy Land, the children of one of the sons of Cush (Nimrod), who settled
in Babylon, Josephus seems to locate the settlements of
the Hamites entirely in Africa.   As we can not in
ancient history locate in Africa any of the descendants
of either Shem or Japheth, we are to consider the
Africans the children of Ham.

But were any of these ancient African nations

colored, or were they white, as Mr. Carroll says? He
states emphatically on page 317 of his book that the
Ethiopians were pure whites. He says this in his effort
to explain the expression "Can the Ethiopian change
his skin, or the leopard his spots?"—Jer. 13:23. He
further says, when commenting upon this text: "There
is absolutely nothing in this text to enable us to de-
termine the complexion of the Ethiopian in the days
of Jeremiah."—Page 315. It is very true that this
text does not describe definitely the complexion of the
Ethiopian—that is, it does not tell us whether he was
black, brown, red, or yellow. The word Ethiopian
might give us a definite idea of this matter, but the
text itself affords proof only that the skin of the Ethiopian was different from the skin of the Israelite. This
is the idea, else the words of the prophet are entirely
without meaning. Why should he use the words,
"Can the Ethiopian change his skin?" if the change
of his skin was not necessary to make him like the
Israelite? If we compare the context we find that
Jeremiah is here comparing the sins of the Israelites to
the skin of the Ethiopian. Let me quote this text
again with a little of its context and see if this is not
the idea Jeremiah meant to convey. "Can the
Ethiopian change his skin, or the leopard his sopts?
then may ye also do good, that are accustomed to do

evil." If the Ethiopian were a white man in the days of Jeremiah, as Mr. Carroll says, to change the Ethiopian's skin would have been a change from white to colored skin, and the text could be read as follows, without changing its sense: "Can the white man change his skin, or the leopard his spots? then may ye also do good, that are accustomed to do evil." This would destroy the sense of the text. But understanding that the Ethiopian had a dark skin, the real meaning of the text appears. If we read the text, "Can the black man change his skin, or the leopard his spots? then may ye do good that are accustomed to do evil," we have a sensible declaration; and we understand the prophet to teach that the Israelites were so bound under their sinful habits and the power of wickedness, that it had become as impossible for them to live right in their sinful condition as it would be for the colored man to make his skin white, or the leopard to dispose of his spots.

Moses' Ethiopian wife is also somewhat of a barrier to Mr. Carroll's theory, but he seems to think that she was not black. Yet it is very evident that something about her was distasteful to Miriam and Aaron, because we are told that they spake against Moses because of the Ethiopian woman whom he had married. Num. 12:1. In his comments upon the marriage of Moses to an Ethiopian woman, Mr. Carroll says: "As has been shown, it was the desire of God that miscegenation should not be practiced; hence he would never have selected as the leader of Israel a degraded amalgamationist with a black wife. The punishments which God visited upon Miriam for her complaint against Moses because he had married an Ethiopian woman proves that the wife of Moses was of pure Adamic stock, and that she was white."—Pages 313, 314.

No, Mr. Carroll, the punishments which God visited upon Miriam for her complaint against Moses are no proof that Moses' wife was white. It would, if God viewed things as you do; but since God has created all the nations of the world, regardless of their color, of one blood, he must convince Miriam of this fact by sending the leprosy upon her for her stout words against the poor black woman that Moses had married.

In another place is a rebuke upon Dr. Talmage for having made reference to Moses' marriage to a colored lady. Mr. Carroll says: "Who but a thoroughly demoralized pulpit advocate of amalgamation, could conceive the absurd idea that God selected a degraded amalgamationist with a black wife to lead to the land of promise the descendants of Abraham, whom he had *chosen for* no other purpose than that they should preserve in its purity and increase the Adamic flesh of the earth, except his designs with reference to the development of the resources of the earth, and the control of the animals, and ultimately destroy the mixed-bloods from the globe." From this harsh language we are enabled to discern the harsh spirit that Mr. Carroll possesses. I would point such spirits to the fountain of the all-cleansing blood of Christ, which will purge from the heart the awful hatred and prejudice existing there against the colored races. The salvation of Christ is a double cure for all this, and will plant love in the heart for all our fellow men, and will enable us, as if by holy X-rays, to see through the dark skins of other races, and like our heavenly Father, accept those in every nation who fear God and work righteousness.

But concerning Moses' wife, who was she? If the wife that Aaron and Miriam spoke against was the daughter of the priest Jethro, she was not of the Ethiopian nation, as in Exod. 2:16 Jethro is plainly called a priest of Midian. The land in which Moses married the daughter of Jethro is called the land of Midian. Ver. 15. The Midianites were not of the nations called in ancient history Ethiopians, but were the descendants of Midian, who was one of the sons of Abraham by his second wife. Gen. 25:1, 2. So this daughter of Jethro whom Moses married was a true daughter of Abraham. If this is the wife that Aaron and Miriam spoke against, we must consider the word Ethiopian to have been applied to this woman because of her complexion. The word Ethiopian is of Greek origin and signifies "burnt face." It was applied to various ancient nations because of their dark complexion. So, if the Ethiopian woman and the Midianite woman, the daughter of Jethro, are identical, Jethro's daughter was called an Ethiopian, not because she belonged to the African nation by that name, but because she was dark complected.

But I am of the opinion that the daughter of Jethro is not the woman that Miriam and Aaron spake against. Josephus tells us that after a great war had been fought between the Egyptians and Ethiopians, in which Moses served the Egyptians as commander-incheif of their armies, and in which the Egyptians were victorious, Moses married the daughter of the king of the Ethiopians, who had fallen in love with him during the Ethiopian war. See "Antiquities," Book 2, Chapter 10. This Ethiopian woman Moses evidently dwelt with until his flight from Egypt into the land of Midian, where he married the daughter of Jethro the priest of Midian. He dwelt with Jethro's daughter *for about forty years*, until God called him to go down into Egypt and bring out his people. When he brought the people out of Egypt he beyond doubt brought his Midianite woman along with the Israelites, and Miriam and Aaron doubtless thought Moses had better left that black woman back in Egypt, and not to have brought her along; but God gave them to understand that the black was only skin deep, and that the blood and inward life of that colored woman was as precious in his sight as that of Aaron and Miriam: and ·gave Miriam to understand that he punished white people when they became haughty, the same as colored people, by giving her a good dose of leprosy that took the healing power of the Lord to deliver her from. I assure you she never spoke against the colored people after that. And I do not think Mr. Carroll would if God should give him a similar dose, which he certainly deserves if Miriam did.

Concerning the colors of the ancient nations, much has been learned from the signification of their names. It is a well-known fact that the Hebrew proper names are all significative. When we observe that many of those names which stand at the head of great nations of antiquity had special reference to the color of those individuals and their descendants, we may form tolerably accurate opinions as regards their color.

We are told in the Bible that Noah had three sons —Shem, Ham, and Japheth. Shem signifies renowned; Ham signifies dark, swarthy; and Japheth signifies fair. So the names of Noah's sons in our language are "Renowned," "Dark," and "Fair." We are told that Adam called his wife's name Eve (that is, life), because she was the mother of all living. He also called her woman (out of man), because she was taken out of man. We also read that the daughter of Pharaoh named the child she found in the vessel upon the water Moses (drawn out), because she had drawn the ark out of the water. Also Isaac named one of his sons Esau (hairy), because he was hairy all over like a woolly blanket. Jacob was named Israel (prevailed with God), because he prevailed with the angel of God. Abram was named Abraham (father of many), because God made him father of many nations. I might thus continue to swell the list of examples in the Bible of names of signification that were given to the various Bible characters because of some particular circumstance or characteristic of the child. May we not reasonably conclude that the names Noah gave to Shem, Ham, and Japheth were such as designated some feature, characteristic, or calling? It is hardly reasonable to suppose that Noah named one *of his* sons Japheth (fair), and another Ham (dark),

if the one was not really fair complected and the other
dark complected. This is a very reasonable conclusion, since similar differences of complexion are ofttimes
witnessed in the same family in our day. The
variation of nature as seen in the complexion of
Japheth and Ham could easily have continued in their
descendants until in the course of a few hundred years
there was a marked distinction between them such
as we see to-day in the Caucasian and Ethiopian races.
It is also highly probable that certain freaks of nature
may have suddenly painted some of Ham's descendants
black.   This is as reasonable as the freak that caused
Esau to be red.   Mr. Carroll can not make out that
the red skin of Esau is a product of amalgamation,
because he was a twin brother to Jacob who was
white. The theory of amalgamation is completely
refuted here.   If we trace the signification of the
names of the children of Ham, we find a freak of nature
that painted one of Ham's children black, just as a
similar freak painted one of Isaac's sons red.

We are told in the tenth chapter of Genesis that
Ham had four sons—Cush, Mizraim, Phut, and
Canaan. The descendants of three of these—Cush,
Mizraim, and Phut—we have seen by Josephus, settled
in Africa, except one of the sons of Cush, Nimrod,
the founder of the city of Babylon, who after the

JACOB AND ESAU.

confusion of tongues remained in that locality. Cush
he told us, was the founder of Ethiopia, Mizraim of
Egypt, and Phut of Lybia. It is unquestionably true
that the Ethiopians were the descendants of Cush. In
our Authorized Version of the scriptures, as well as in
the LXX., they are called Ethiopians; but in the Hebrew
scriptures they are always called Cushites. Josephus
tells us that the Ethiopians were still called Cushites
by the people who dwelt in Asia. This is beyond doubt
true, for the Peshitto Version of the New Testament,
a Syriac version that was translated from the Greek
later than the time of Josephus, still retains the name
of Cushites for the Ethiopians. In that version we
read of the eunuch of Acts 8:27 as follows: "And
there he met a eunuch who had come from Cush, an
officer of Candace queen of the Cushites, who had
charge of all her treasure." The land of Ethiopia is
here called Cush. It is so denominated always in the
Hebrew Bible. If we examine the word Cush we can
find in it some proof that the Ethiopians were a
dark-skinned people. The word Cush signifies black;
and why should Ham name one of his sons *Black* if he
were not very dark complected? If we translate the
word Cush by its true signification we will have the
Ethiopians spoken of in the Bible as follows:

"And Miriam and Aaron spoke against Moses because

of the black woman whom he had married; for he had married a black woman."—Num. 12:1.

"So the Lord smote the black men before Asa and before Judah, and the black men fled. . . And the black men were overthrown that they could not recover themselves; for they were destroyed before the Lord, and before his host."—2 Chron. 14:12, 13.

"So shall the king of Assyria lead away the Egyptians captives, and the black men captives, young and old."—Isa. 20:4.

"Can the black man change his skin, or the leopard his spots? then may y also do good, that are accustomed to do evil."—Jer. 13:23.

It is thus that the Hebrew Bible talks about the Ethiopians. It never calls them anything else but blacks. The father of these Ethiopians was called black; his children were always called black people; and the country in which they dwelt was always called the land of the blacks. When the Hebrews read in their Bible that Moses had married a black woman, they understood all about her complexion; and when they read from Jeremiah, "Can the black man change his skin?" there was no parleying among them as to whether the Ethiopians were black or white. They knew exactly what it meant; for their Scriptures conveyed exactly the same idea that these scriptures do as I have translated them above.

But Mr. Carroll might argue that this name "Black" was only applied to the descendants of Cush because his name was Cush. We might reason this way, were it not for some other things which go to show that the name was perpetuated because the descendants of Cush were black like himself. The name Ethiopian is one of more recent origin than the word Cushite. It is of Greek origin and signifies "sun-burnt face." It is formed out of *aithomai* (to burn) and *ops* (the face). This name was given to the Cushites by the Greeks. Why should the Greeks call those people "sun-burnt faces," if they were not dark-skinned people? So it is very evident that the Hebrew name Cush and the Greek name Ethiopian were applied to the descendants of the first son of Ham because they were dark-skinned people. Mr. Carroll can not evade these facts.

It might be well to observe also that there were very many dark-skinned people in ancient times, besides those who dwelt in the country of Ethiopia; hence the words Cush, among the Hebrews, and Ethiopian, among the Greeks, were used in an extended sense to designate any or all of the black-skinned tribes of ancient times. Kitto, in his Cyclopedia of Biblical Literature, concerning the word Ethiopia, says: "As used among the Greeks and Romans the word was employed in all the latitude of its etymological meaning, to denote any of the countries where the people are of a sable sunburnt complexion." The word Cush also among the Hebrews was used in an extended sense similar to the use of the word Ethiopian among the Greeks and Romans, and they used it to designate other black nations besides the Ethiopians of Africa. In Gen. 2: 13 is a reference to another land of Cush (Ethiopia), which was compassed by the river Gihon, one of the rivers that flowed out of the garden of Eden. This land of Cush, or Ethiopia, was a long ways from the African Ethiopia. This is a proof that the word Cush was applied to more than one country and to more than one class of people, by the Hebrews. Doubtless it was used in the same sense that the word Ethiopian was used among the Greeks and Romans, and the use of the word was, as stated above, governed by the complexion of various nations. So Mr. Carroll can not get around the fact that the black race has descended largely from Ham, and to this day they are found chiefly in the land that was taken up by Ham's descendants: but they are not found there exclusively; they are in other parts of the world. So it is doubtless true that some of the Negroes are descendants of Shem and Japheth, because these variations of nature are seen among them as well as the Hamites. It is a fact well demonstrated that the Egyptians, Ethiopians, and Canaanites, who beyond possibility of doubt were the descendants of Ham, were all dark-skinned; but the Ethiopians were the darkest. The Lybians were dark, but more fair than the rest of Ham's descendants. The Phœnicians were descendants of Ham, and are said to have been of a reddish color. The word Phœnician seems to signify *red man*. The Phœnicians were a great empire in ancient times and founded, we are told, three hundred cities upon the western coast of Africa. They also founded Carthage in northern Africa, and two hundred cities upon the coast of Spain. They founded also Tarsus, another great city of ancient times, which, according to the claim that generally prevails, was situated on the coast of Spain. The descendants of these red men—the dark-skinned Egyptians, the black Ethiopians, and the swarthy Lybians—are the ancestors of the present African nations; and there is no getting around the fact. So when Mr. Carroll states so emphatically in his book that the Negroes are not descendants of Ham, he either ignores the many historical evidences there are against him, or is ignorant of the fact that they exist.

CIVILIZATION.

Mr. Carroll holds that the colored races are not capable of a high state of civilization. All the highly civilized nations of antiquity he affirms to have been fair-skinned tribes. He says:

"When we turn upon these ancient civilizations the light of the sciences, we find they were the work of the whites. No Negro civilization has ever appeared. No Mongolian one has ever greatly developed. The white is preeminently the man of civilization. This is just what God created him to be. The mixed-bloods may inherit from their Adamic ancestors their knowledge of the arts and sciences, but they are almost certain to lose it; and, when lost, it is lost to them forever; they have no ability to replace it. Many valuable arts which these ancient whites possessed were inherited by their mixed-blooded descendants and lost; such as the art of tempering copper to the hardness of steel, etc. In every case we find the remains of these ancient civilizations in the hands of red, brown, and yellow populations, which, in the sum of their characters, are identical with the known offspring of whites and Negroes in our midst. In addition to this our personal observation, sustained by the most intelligent scientific research, teaches that the only way to produce a brown, red, or yellow-complexioned individual is to mingle the blood of the white with that of the Negro."—Pages 234, 235.

These words of our author contain several assertions that he can not prove. To say that civilization has always been confined within the limits of the Caucasian race, is grossly absurd, especially since we have a number of civilized nations among the colored races at the present time. Also in ancient times there were many civilized nations among the colored races, as well as civilized and barbarous nations of the Caucasian race. The ancient Egyptians, Ethiopians, Lybians, and Canaanites were all highly civilized, yet we have well-grounded reasons for saying they all belonged to the colored races. The Encyclopedia Britannica, under Anthropology, says: "The color of the skin has always been held as specially distinctive. The colored race portraits of ancient Egypt remain to prove the permanence of complexion during the lapse of a hundred generations, distinguishing coarsely but clearly the types of the red-brown Egyptian, the yellow-brown Canaanite, the comparatively fair Lybian, and the Negro."

We have before shown that the Ethiopians were a

colored people; so we have here, beyond doubt, four colored civilized nations of antiquity; and I think we can not justly doubt that the Phœnicians were also a colored people. So, Mr. Carroll is mistaken in his idea that colored races can not develop civilizations. Mr. Carroll admits that the ruins of ancient civilizations are found in the hands of the colored races, but asserts, without attaching any proof to his saying, that they belong, not to these colored races, but, to whites of some remote period. This must be treated as a presumption of our author. He has no shadow of evidence in favor of his opinion that at one time the entire world was peopled by whites, who owned and worked Negroes as slaves. There is no historical nor scientific evidence to prove his theory. It stands alone upon the word of our author. The evidences are against his theory. If the whites once dwelt in every clime and owned Negroes as domestic animals, and afterwards descended to amalgamation with them, the entire world of to-day would be peopled with mixed-bloods. But this is not the case. Many nations are all pure Caucasian and bear no traces of dark skins, and yet do not own any Negroes. In other parts of the world there are nations composed exclusively of people with black skins, with no trace of whites, reds, browns, or yellows. In these cases what became of the original whites and blacks? Again, if the world was once peopled with whites, who owned and worked Negroes as slaves, and who afterwards descended to amalgamation with them, how can we account for the fact that about half of the world's population to-day are Caucasians, and that the Negro race constitutes a very small per cent. of the inhabitants of the world? I think it would be difficult for Mr. Carroll to present a reasonable explanation of these facts which are in opposition to his theory.

If we consider the barbarity of antiquity, the colored nations are on a par with the whites. Many of the highest civilized Caucasian nations of to-day have arisen out of the lowest kind of barbarity. They have come up out of polygamy, sodomy, cannibalism, fornication, adultery, superstition, and idolatry. Mr. Carroll denies that the white race has ever practiced cannibalism; but if we are to believe the testimonies of the early Christian fathers, this evil prevailed even among the Scots. "The early Christian writers frequently attributed cannibalism to the unconverted Pagans. St. Jerome gives his personal testimony to the practice, stating that when he was a little boy living in Gaul, he beheld the Scots—a people of Britain—eating human flesh; and though there were plenty of cattle and sheep *at their* disposal, yet would they prefer a ham of the

herdsman or a piece of female breast as a luxury."-
Alden's Cyclopedia, Cannibalism.

But cannibalism is not always a proof of degradation
of the deepest dye. Concerning this fact the same
work a little below says: "The facts, however, which
we possess, show that the people systematically
addicted to human flesh are not the most degraded of
the human race. For instance, in the Australian continent where the larger animals are scarce, the people,
who are of an extremely degraded type, feed on herbs
and worms, and have been known only in casual and
exceptional conditions to feed on human flesh. The
New Zealanders, on the other hand, the most highly
developed aboriginal race with which late European
civilization has had to compete, were, till recently,
systematic feeders on human flesh, despising the in-
efficient food which satisfies the natives of Australia."

Leaving the people of antiquity, let us come to
modern civilization. Look at the rapid progress being made in Japan. Few examples of more rapid progress in civilization are upon record, than that which
that nation of Mongolians is making. The world is
looking upon her and her rapid progress with amaze-
ment. Let us look at the poor, persecuted African
Negro himself in our own country. He was imported
from the depths of barbarism in Africa and has dwelt

among the American people a little less than three hundred years. The greater part of this time he has been owned by the white man, as a horse or other domestic animal, and has had about the same chance of mental development that the horse has had. For thirty-five years he has been considered a citizen of our country; but there are few places where the prejudice of the whites against him has not curtailed his rights as a citizen. His citizenship has never been on a par with the white. He has not had the same opportunity that the whites have had to educate himself. It is true there has been an honest Christian sentiment in his favor in some places, which has caused the organization of societies that have raised funds for the purpose of assisting the freed man in his educational pursuits; but, on the other hand, there has been a far stronger sentiment against his progress, and that has ever endeavored to hold the Negro below the level of the white citizens. Yet, notwithstanding these hindrances to the advancement of the colored race in America, they have made a marked progress. The following statistics from a history of the Negro race show how the onward and upward progression of the freed man is accelerated in our midst.

"The gigantic growth of the Negro race in the *United States* from A. D. 1620 to 1900, amounting in population to about 10,000,000 persons, with a proficient constituency of this number, representing the race in every professional and business pursuit carried on by the American nation, has caused the whole world to wonder at its rapid advancement, ability and potency in civilization. In thirty-four years the race has wiped out forty-five per cent. of its illiteracy, and now has 17,311 students in the higher institutions of learning (i. e., in high schools and colleges):

15,008 Negro teachers.

13,581 youths learning trades.

2,410 pursuing classical courses.

974 pursuing scientific courses.

974 pursuing business courses.

22,000 graduates.

224,794 volumes in school libraries.

176 universities, colleges, normal and high schools (approximately).

909 Negro doctors.

5 banks.

156 newspapers.

4 magazines.

4 denominational publishing houses.

1,400 books and publications by colored authors.

$26,626,448 in church property.

Owns 264,000 farms and homes.

Owns $14,000,000 worth of property in the one state of Georgia.

Like the Phoenix in the ancient fables, the Negro race has revived quickly from the tyrannical oppression, ignorance, and superstition to which slavery and bondage had reduced it, and during the short period of thirty-four years has by thrift, industry, sobriety, and Christian piety attained such magnitude, that the world with its crowned heads, nobles, statesmen, and chief dignitaries must acknowledge the greatness of the American Negro."

We should not consider the preceding as the progress of three hundred years. No; it is the progress of thirty-five years. When the slaves were freed they were all illiterate, and, as above stated, since that time there have been great currents of opposition to their advancement. Since, therefore, they have in so short a time climbed to those heights against the greatest tides of opposition, shall we, after the advice of Mr. Carroll, tramp beneath our feet this race which is struggling against the tides of opposition to advance itself to the heights of civilization, and again bring these freed men down to the level of the brute creation and make them our slaves? Surely every lover of civilization whose heart is not filled with prejudice against a man because his skin is black, will say to the freed man,

"Go on" and will assist him in every way he finds it possible to improve his mental development, and thus make him a better and nobler citizen of our beloved country.

But Mr. Carroll argues that we can never make him a respectable citizen, and refers us to the black villain who waylays the unsuspecting traveler, ravishes the daughters of the South, and fills our land with crime, as a proof of his argument. But we must remember that some of those black villains are covered with white skins, and that many who are black outwardly are respectable and pure-spirited lovers of civilization and order. It is true that in many parts of the country the majority of the crimes are committed by Negroes; but how could it be otherwise, when in those same localities where the most of the crimes are committed by Negroes, the Negro has but very little chance to make of himself a respectable citizen? In many of these places the colored people are barred out of the schools, not by law, but by the public sentiment. If we expect to stop the crimes of the Negroes, we must use the same means that we would apply to the white criminals—we must teach them to be something and to make something of themselves in this world. We can never do this except we give them the most careful attention.

But you would remark: "The colored man is far beneath the white in civilization." If this be true, we should give him the greater attention. We should help those who are most in need of help. Since the colored man has so recently sprung out of barbarism, he needs our assistance in his efforts to civilize himself, more than the white race, and we can help him without neglecting our own race. We can educate both races and bring them up to a state of respectability that will greatly lessen crime in our midst. The Negro above all the citizens of our country should be assisted in his progress in civilization and Christianity. We should study him and find where lie the hindrances to his progress and then help him to remove them. We should not allow ourselves to be menaced by that feeling of jealousy which is so manifest in some parts of the country.

The greatest hindrance to the progress of the Negro race among us in morality and civilization is the liquor traffic It is a great curse to the white population, but it is a greater curse to the colored people. I have carefully watched the influence the liquor traffic has over the colored people, and I am certain that it is much more difficult for them as a rule to limit themselves in the use of intoxicating liquors than the *whites.* I. have rarely seen a colored drinking man

whose drinking habits were not limited by his pocket-
book only. Many of them work hard in the factories and
mines, and never retain possession of a single cent
longer than it will take them to drink it up. They
live out of the employers' stores, and on pay day their
store bills are deducted from their wages, and of
course the Negro draws the remainder of his pay. He
then goes directly to the saloon, where he remains
until his money is gone. Many of them never go
home from the mines to wash on pay day, but go to
the saloon and wash themselves, and there bum until
their money is gone.

Many white men also have this same habit, but the
Negro shows the lesser power of restraint. It is our
duty as American citizens to remove this abominable
curse; when it has been removed, the greatest hindrance to the moral advancement of the colored race
in our midst will have been removed.

What assistance does Mr. Carroll hope to lend to the
advancement of the world in civilization by his book?
Does he hope to increase the friendship and love of the
nations for each other by teaching them that some of
them only are men, and that others are apes, and others
a mixture between man and the ape? Does he hope
to break down the great prejudice in the hearts of the
whites *in our* country against the Negro by telling the

white that the Negro is not a man? Does he hope to
raise the Negro to a higher plane by telling him that
he is not .. man, that he has no soul, that he is on a
par with the horse, that death ends all to him? Does
he hope to stop the tide of amalgamation, which he
denounces in so strong terms, by teaching the white
males that the Negroes are not human beings—that
they are not his equal? The very opinion existing in
the white males that Negroes are not their equal and
have not equal rights with them as citizens, is the
prime cause of the amalgamation between the whites
and the Negroes. Give the white young man to understand that the Negro is a human being as well as himself and a citizer of the United States of America and
on a par with himself, and that the Negro young
woman justly merits a par citizenship with himself,
and give the Negro woman also to understand that she
has a right to a par citizenship with the white
man and the greater part of the amalgamation will
have ceased. At the present time, notwithstanding
the laws of our country which make the Negro a par
citizen with the Caucasian the tradition exists in
many parts of the country that the Negro has no right
to a par citizenship with the white; and irrespective
of the laws and constitution of the United States he
is debarred from his rights as a citizen, and is looked

upon as being but little above the domestic animals. Consequently the white whoremonger thinks he has a right to use those colored women as he pleases, and so after night in many of the cities of the United States the color line is completely obliterated. In this way nearly all of the amalgamation is carried on. I am not an advocate of amalgamation, and I am sure that the better classes of both races do not favor it. If the male part of the white race should be made to understand that they will be held responsible by the laws of the states and punished just as severely for the seduction of a black woman as of a white woman, they will take care how they molest the colored women.

It is the continual cry of those whose hearts are filled with the race prejudice, that we must keep the colored man down. We must not allow him equal rights with the whites, or our country will soon be drenched in amalgamation. But this is a mistake. The colored race has ever been held down, and yet the country is flooded with amalgamation. And how is it brought about? It is not by allowing the colored race their rights as citizens, for statistics will show that in places where the Negro enjoys the greatest privileges as a free citizen of America, the per cent. of amalgamation is the lowest; and in places where he enjoys the least privileges as an American citizen, the per cent. of amalgamation is the highest. The reason of this is: where the colored people are considered human in every respect they are treated so; and where they are not considered first-class human beings, they are treated so. In a few states there are no laws even against the marriage of the blacks and whites, yet in these states the per cent. of amalgamation runs very low, because both races are educated, and a colored man when set to thinking is as much opposed to amalgamation as a white man; consequently it is a rare thing in these states to find a mixture of the blood of the two races. In some states the strictest laws are enacted against the marriage of the whites and blacks, and the blacks are in every way isolated from the society of the whites. In such states generally the race prejudice runs very high, and the colored man is considered to be little if any above the brute creation; yet, notwithstanding all this precaution (they say it is all intended as a precaution against amalgamation) the per cent. of amalgamation is the highest. I hold that the prime cause of this lies in the fact that the colored man is kept down.

The illiterate colored people of to-day, being the first and second generations of the children of the slaves, who just a few generations back migrated from a *low state* of barbarism, having no culture nor training in civilization, except what they incidentally gathered from their association with the white race, can not be expected to have very exalted views of morality; consequently they will not look upon adultery as a very great sin.   The male part of the white race, being taught that the colored race are mere brutes—apes— as Mr. Carroll would have it, or perhaps only a step higher than the brute—as some will allow—will, as a natural consequence, look upon the abolition of the color-line after dark for the purpose of gratifying his sensuality as no sin.   This I believe to be a true diagnosis of amalgamation in our country; and I hold that I am advocating the only doctrine that will prove a success to any extent as a preventative of it.

LaVergne, TN USA
05 April 2010
178206LV00001B/136/A

9 781432 675943